Custom Bikes

FROM FACTORY TO FANTASY

Edited by **Volker Koerdt**

COURAGE BOOKS

AN IMPRINT OF
RUNNING PRESS BOOK PUBLISHERS
Philadelphia • London

© 1994 Transedition Books, a division of Andromeda Oxford Limited

© 1992 Motorbuch Verlag

First published in the United States of America by Running Press Book Publishers.

This book may not be reproduced in whole or in part, in any form or by any means, electronic or mechanical, including photocopying, recording or by any information storage and retrieval system now known or hereafter invented, without written permission from the publisher.

9 8 7 6 5 4 3 2 1

Digit on the right indicates the number of this printing.

Library of Congress Cataloging-in-Publication Number 94-65113

ISBN 1-56138-478-X

Printed in Spain.

Published by Courage Books, an imprint of
Running Press Book Publishers
125 South Twenty-second Street
Philadelphia, Pennsylvania 19103-4399

Contents

Introduction	5
Naumann Ducati	6
Klein Moto Guzzi	12
Bambach BMW	18
Laibacher Ducati	24
Gaßebner Honda	30
Flink-Egli Suzuki	36
Derleth Honda	42
Diko 500	48
Sera Kawasaki	54
Heinemeyer Kawasaki	60
R M C Suzuki	66
Luscher Yamaha	72
BoT Harley-Davidson	78
Erla Special	84
Schneider Adler	90

Introduction

Many motorcyclists experience with their machines not only the joys of riding, but also the delights of tinkering. Given the technical know-how, the urge to personalize their vehicle is more marked among bikers than in any other group of motor enthusiasts. This book, with its fine color illustrations, is ample evidence of that.

Since the German motorcycling magazine PS – Das Sport Motorradmagazin first introduced a custom bike in its pages at the beginning of 1989, all kinds of machines have appeared in individual issues: from racing bikes to choppers, enduros, and classic bikes, of Italian, Japanese, American and German make. The constructors have always presented their marvellous two-wheeled creations in immaculate condition.

As time went by, a real competition developed among the custom bikers who wanted to have their machines featured. More beauty, more refinement and more perfection were their aims as they prepared their machines, often in years of painstaking work. In this book of custom bikes we have brought together the best examples from the last few years, many of them easily worth five-figure sums. In doing this, the editors have taken a close look not only at the technical features of these fine machines, but also at the people behind the bikes, people who were born with a wrench in their hand. Last but not least, this book of custom bikes is not only a treasure trove for technical buffs, but also a delight to the eye, thanks to the excellent quality of its photography.

Volker Koerdt, Editor

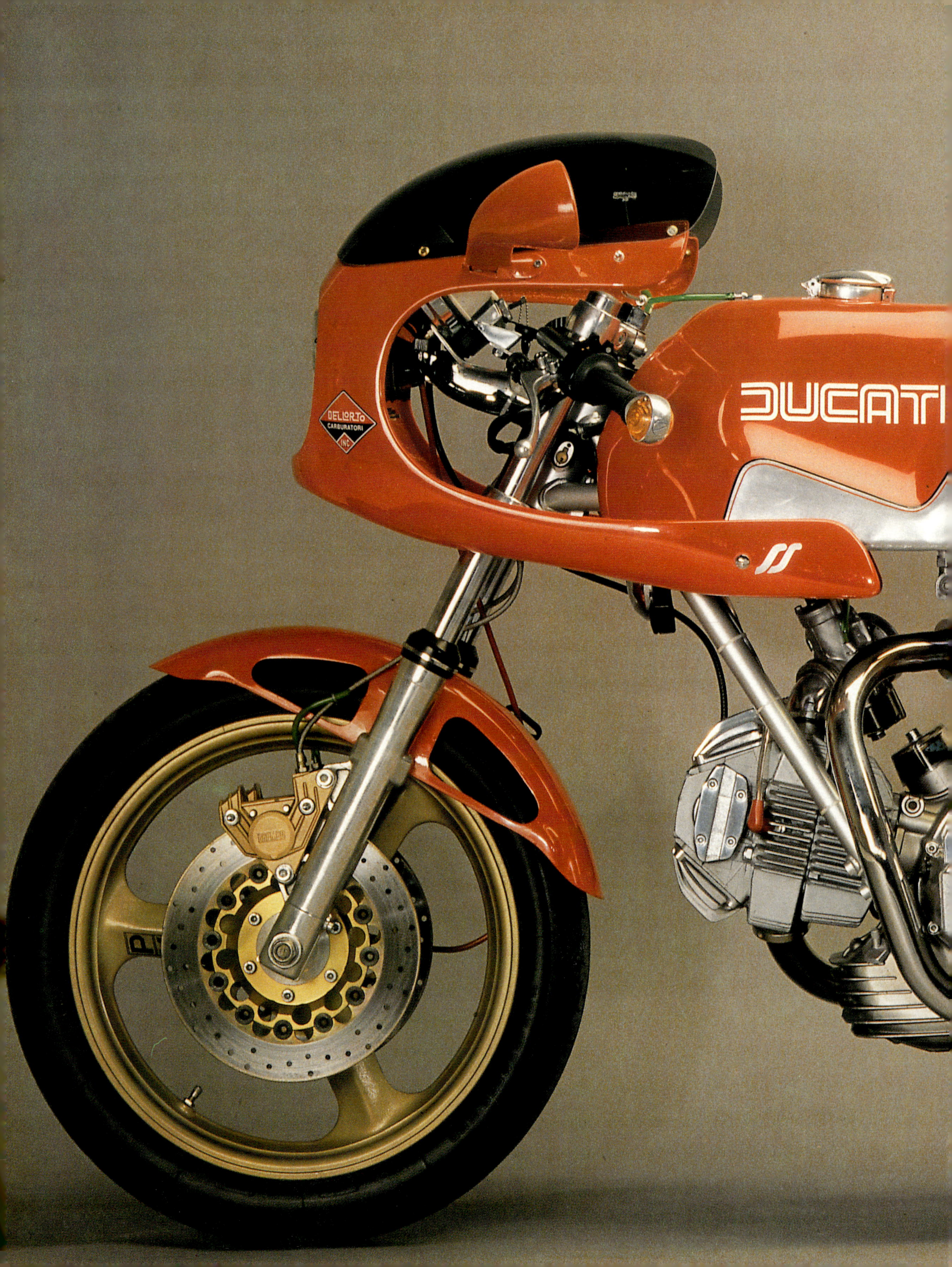
DUCATI
DELLORTO
CARBURATORI

Hard Beat

When a Ducati V-twin blasts out its hard, torquey beat through open Conti pipes, it's not only fans of the Bolognese maker who feel their hearts beat faster.

NZR

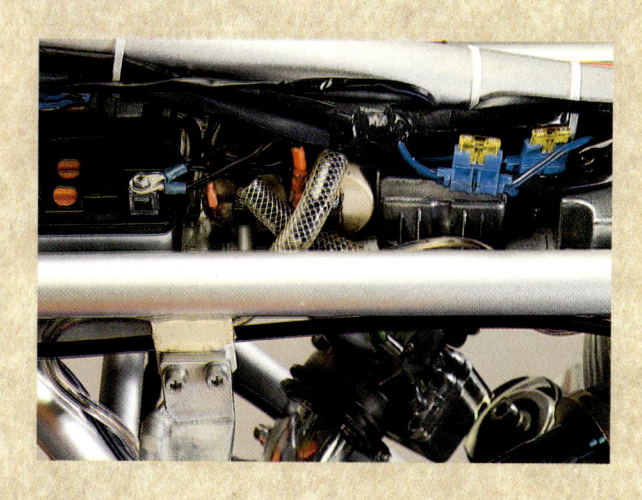

There she stands, a thrilling sight in gleaming red, with her big, shiny heart open for all to see, since the narrow Harris fairing with its two bright eyes hides nothing of the V-twin masterpiece underneath. You'll need a sensitive touch if you want to hear its beat at the first encounter. Carefully tap the two Dell'Orto 41 racing carbs to fill them with the vital juice, and give her four or five nudges of the kickstarter. Then the observer quickly becomes a listener: the hard beat from the Conti pipes blends with the gurgling of the carburation. Anyone who has any doubts about the way the engine sounds can check up on the working of the camshaft through a porthole, which gives a clear view of the rotating bevel gears. Klaus Naumann, motor mechanic and builder of the customized Ducati, didn't put in the Perspex window above the camshaft

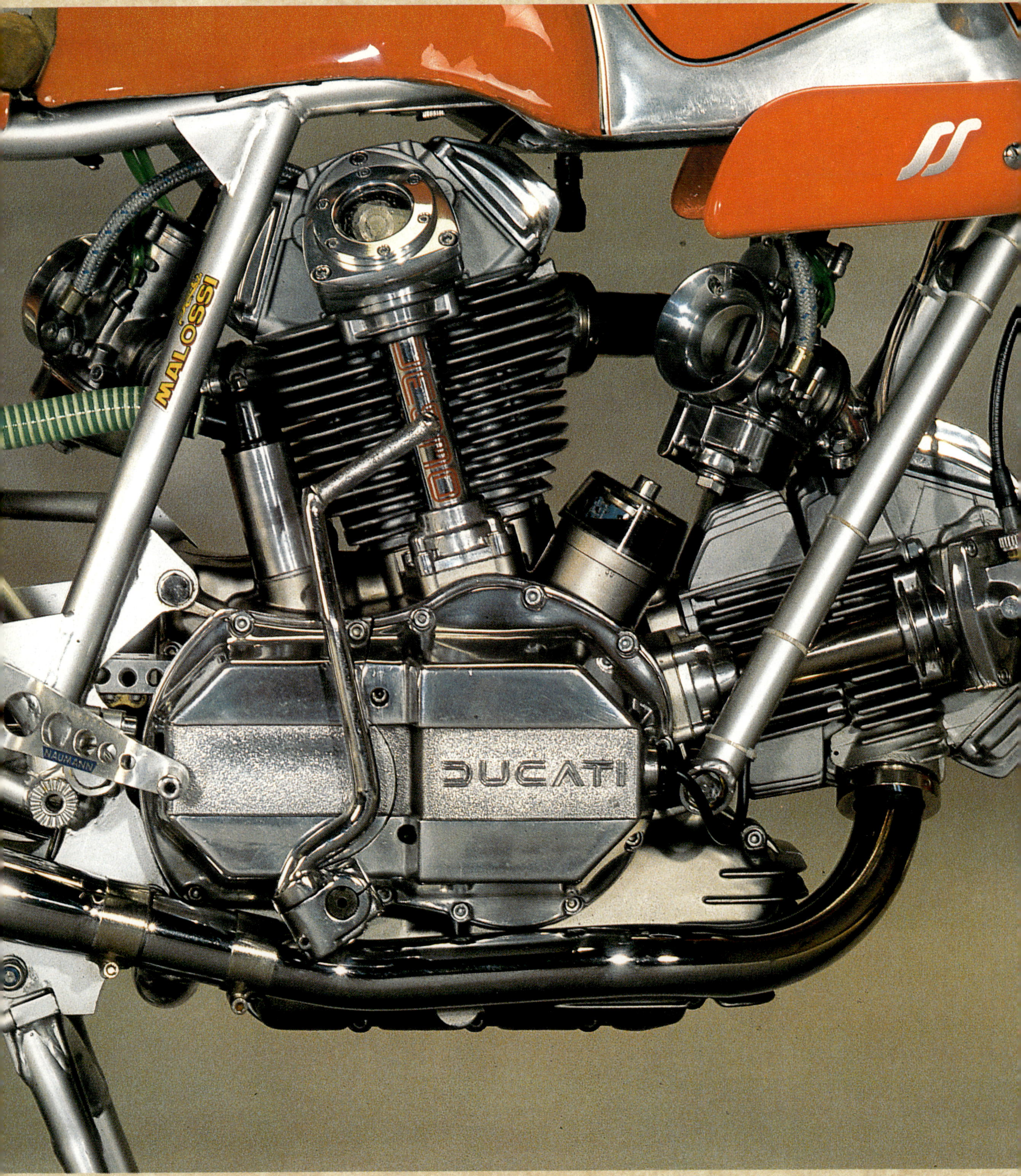
MALOSSI
NAUMANN
DUCATI

drive simply for the sake of appearances; when starting from cold, it allows him to see if the rather feeble oil-pump has delivered any lubricant to the cylinder head. Naumann acquired the badly run-down 1979 Ducati 900 in the fall of 1987; the conversion took a year and cost $6,500.

DATA SHEET

Engine	Air-cooled V-twin four-stroke
Bore & Stroke	3.4 x 2.9 in (86 x 74.4 mm)
Capacity	53 cu ins (864 cc)
Power	75 bhp at 7,500 rpm
Transmission	Five-speed gearbox
Wheelbase	59 ins (1500 mm)
Frame	Tubular steel frame
Weight	440 lb (200 kg) with full tank
Maximum speed	141 mph (225 kph)
Production year	1979
Constructor	Klaus Naumann/Ducati

11

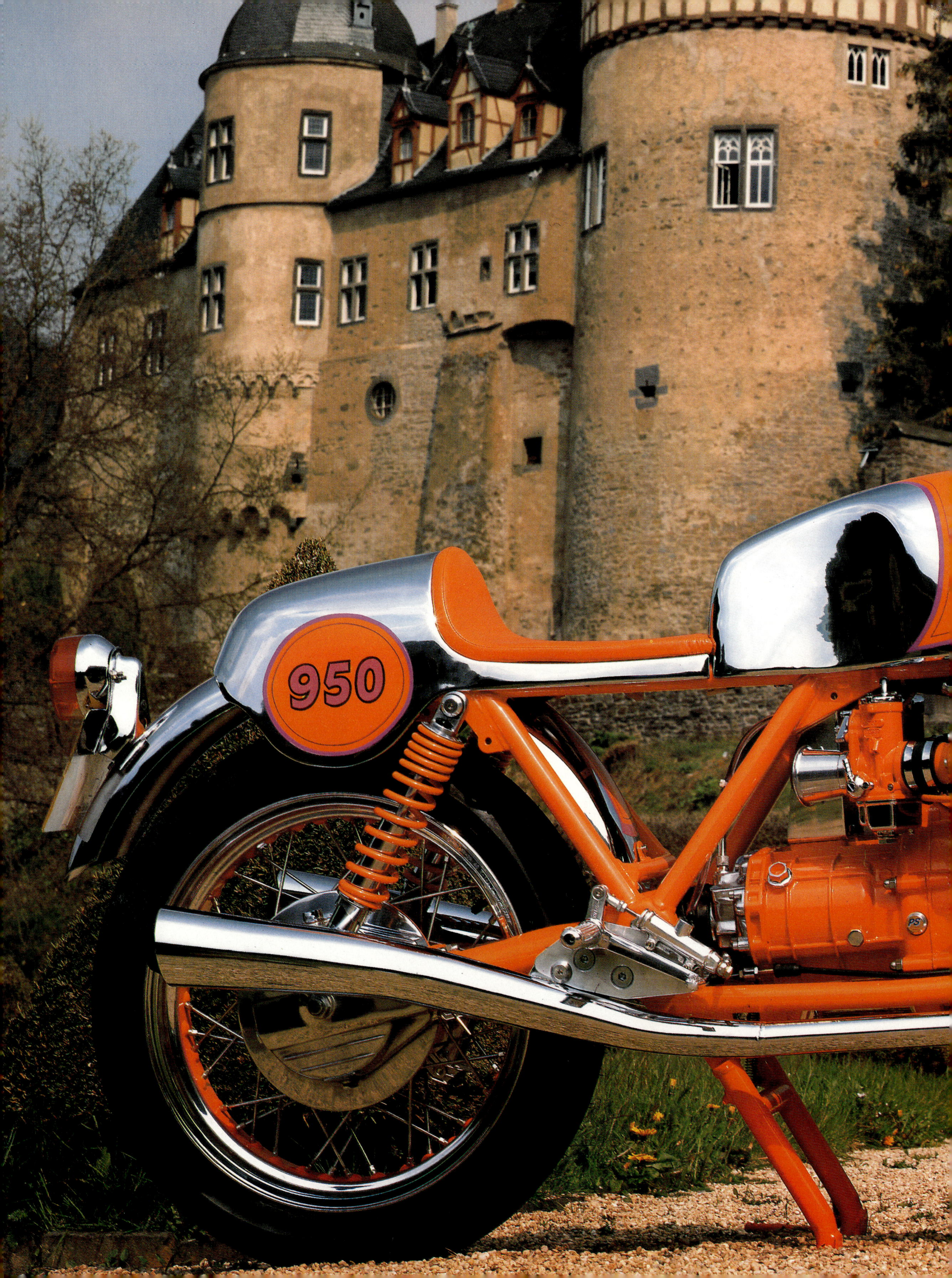
950

Vision in Orange

From time to time, cost controller Gerhard Klein swaps his red pencil for a designer's pen. Here he has put together a colorful piece of machinery, in the middle of which sits the mighty Moto Guzzi V-twin.

Managers generally suffer from stress. This is certainly the case with the builder of this custom bike. During the week he oversees with meticulous care the finances of a large automobile manufacturer which has any number of engines, from four to eight cylinders, on its list. On the weekends he

14

prefers to devote himself, with the same thoroughness, to twin-cylinder two-wheelers. The man in question is Gerhard Klein. "I haven't really got any time for riding, and less still for doing up nuts and bolts. But every now and again I just make the time for myself. Then I sit down, draw a design, and eventually get started on the mechanical work." This time he took a Moto Guzzi as his subject, in order to show us what can be done, both technically and in terms of appearance. Out of two Moto Guzzi Le Mans he made, over many hundreds of hours, a classic racer which has a trick or two up its cylinders.

The result was a V-twin prima donna from Mandello, on which Klein had spared no expense. He had the capacity of the Moto Guzzi Le

Mans II engine increased by Newton Equipment of London to 57 cu ins (940 cc), while larger valves and polished induction tracts allow it to breathe properly. At the same time, the Newton team made the engine more robust, with a lightened and polished crankshaft, balanced pistons, and outrageously expensive Carillo titanium connecting rods.

The perfectionist owner built up the running gear around the frame of a Le Mans IV. It was sprayed with a specially made powder coating before assembly. Chromed 18-inch spoked wheels, a Marzocchi 40 fork, and Koni telescopic arms completed the superior chassis. Two non-floating Brembo Serie d'Oro calipers grip the front wheel's twin Spondon discs. Our fan of all things Italian was prepared to leave the original brake system at the rear. "But I simply had to have Hi-Sport radials," says Klein, "so that I can really enjoy the endlessly twisting roads in Tuscany, where I'm going on holiday." The Klein Guzzi is also a joy to behold. Tank, seat pan and mudguards are hand-beaten custom-made parts, made of steel and polished before receiving the layers of nickel and chrome which give them a lasting high gloss. The

DATA SHEET

Engine	Air-cooled V-twin four-stroke
Bore & Stroke	3.5 x 3 ins (88 x 78 mm)
Capacity	57 cu ins (950 cc)
Power	75 bhp at 7,300 rpm
Transmission	Five-speed gearbox
Wheelbase	59 ins (1495 mm)
Frame	Double cradle steel tubular frame
Weight	407 lb (185 kg) with full tank
Maximum speed	122 mph (195 kph)
Production year	1990
Constructor	Gerhard Klein/Moto Guzzi

absolutely perfect paintwork comes, in Klein's words, from "the legendary masters of the trade" – Woodings of Ashford, England.

Anyone who thinks that in spite of this the paint on the engine might flake off at some time, and that the Guzzi can only be for show, will be proved wrong. The engine block, which is heat-resistant up to 752° F (400° C), was developed specially for Klein's project by the Saarbrücken company Dr. Becker & Co. It can be relied on to keep its beautiful finish even in the heat of everyday traffic. Klein really does want to ride his Guzzi, in order to enjoy its colorful character to the full.

BMW Boxer fights on

"They never come back" goes the old boxer's saying – but when a true BMW freak has been at work night after night, even an old police BMW can pack a real punch.

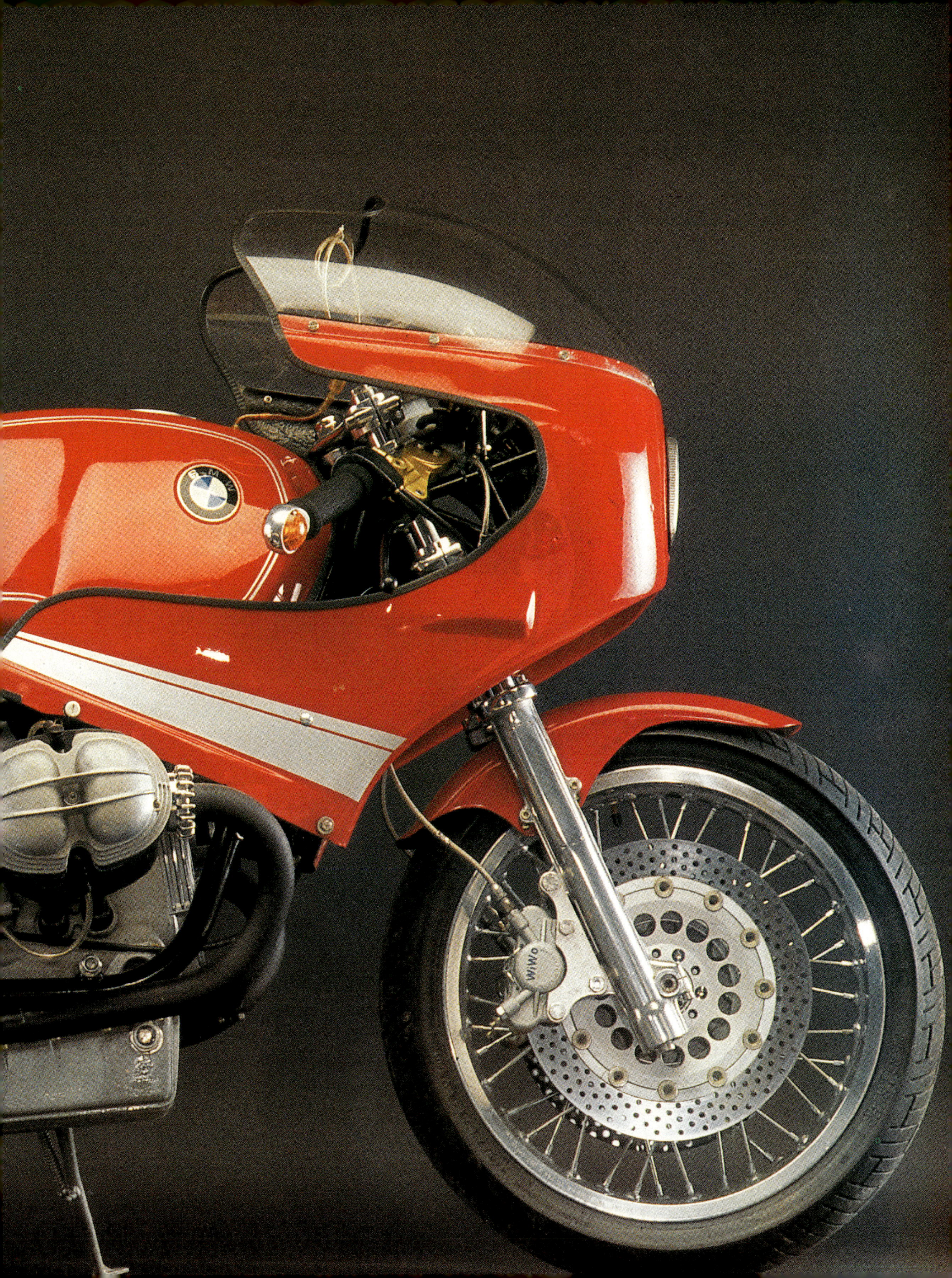
BMW

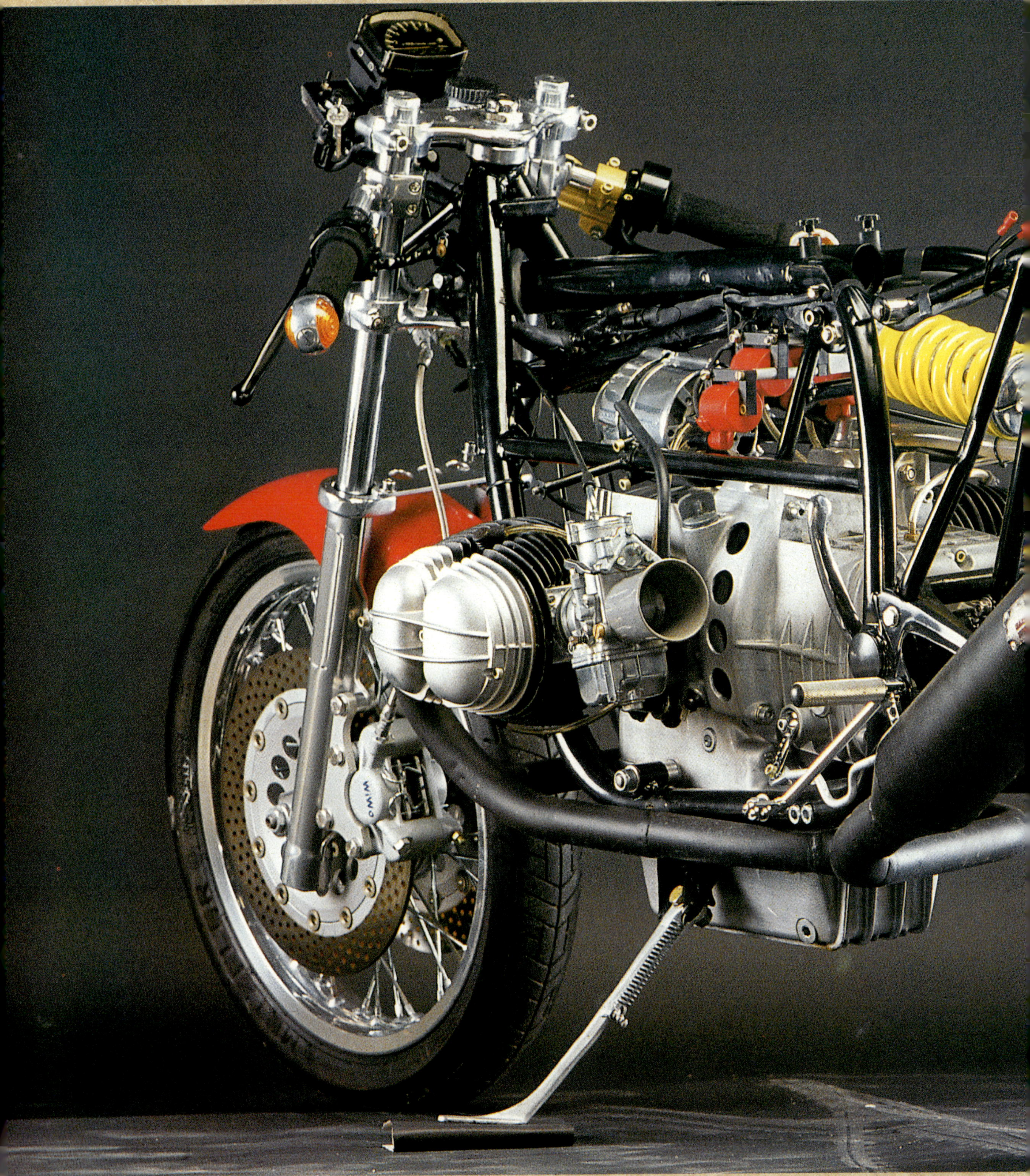

If, after years of official duty, a modest 1974 police BMW is to begin a second career as a performance machine, you've got to do more than strip off the old police fairing. Andreas Bambach was having no half measures; on his R90/6 only the tank, parts of the engine housing, and one piece of the frame are

21

standard. Now this flat twin or "boxer"-engined bike weighs in as a lightweight – at 409 lb (186 kg) ready for the road – and packs a well-tuned 86 bhp. The cantilever chassis is one of the early models from Völkel's, the frame specialists. An additional strut between the frame spine and the gearbox casing distributes the forces that the monoshock swinging arm feeds into the frame. The bottom tubes of the double cradle frame can be unscrewed, and stiffening struts have been welded into the cradle tubes to right and left, above the cylinders. The Bilstein shock absorber is fitted with a special spring with a 4-inch travel. The fork is custom-made using parts from 14 different BMW models: shortened R90S stanchions, stiffer springs, modified shock absorbers, plus sliders from the R100S, and an alloy upper fork yoke instead of the original sheet steel part.

Complementing these are WiWo 320 twin disc brakes, and wire wheels with 18-inch alloy rims. Because of the fat rear tire (a Metzeler MBS 150/70 V18), the engine is slightly offset in the frame and the rear wheel is dished to one side. Crankshaft and connecting rods are lightened, finely balanced, and polished, as are the rockers, valves, and pushrods. A camshaft with 75 thou (1.9 mm) more lift and stiffer valve springs allow over 8,000 rpm. Electronic twin ignition and a two-into-one exhaust give plentiful performance.

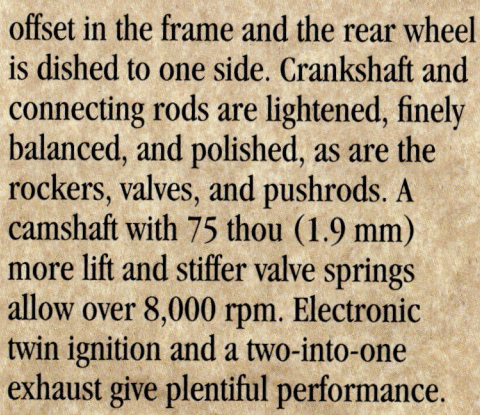

DATA SHEET

Engine	Air-cooled flat twin four-stroke
Bore & Stroke	3.7 x 2.7 ins (94 x 70.6 mm)
Capacity	60 cu ins (980 cc)
Power	86 bhp at 8,000 rpm
Transmission	Five-speed gearbox
Wheelbase	56.7 ins (1440 mm)
Frame	Double cradle frame
Weight	409 lb (186 kg)
Maximum speed	131 mph (210 kph)
Production year	1974, rebuilt 1989
Constructor	Andreas Bambach/BMW

Yvonne's rival

If banker Jörg Laibacher isn't busy with his girlfriend Yvonne, he'll be working on his Ducati F1. The result is appreciated by all.

DUCATI
J. Laibacher
verlicchi
Desmo
UCATI
Tel. 07192 / 7817
LANDSGESELL · WERBUNG & DESIGN
LAAUSER
Design International
diadora
MARVIC

"Without the understanding of my girlfriend Yvonne, who put up with me doing all the grinding and polishing work in our flat, my dream Ducati could never have become reality," confesses banker Jörg Laibacher, whose other great passion is for the mighty twins from Bologna and coaxing not only performance but also a rich sound from their two cylinders, by means of desmodromic valve gear, huge carburetors exhaust pipes as thick as your arm. For this Ducati freak a standard Duke was out of the question; he had to have something unique.

For this reason the F1 which he bought in 1989 had to shed a whole load of standard parts. To the cylinder heads Laibacher fitted 1x inch (42 mm) inlet and 1x inch (38 mm) exhaust valves, hardened valve seats for use with lead-free gasoline, and twin ignition. An 11:1 compression ratio, hotter cams from NCR with increased lift, and pistons with modified cutaways for the valves keep the racing twin running sweetly. The two cylinders are fed by 1.6 inch Mallossi carburetors and exhausted by a NCR two-into-one system with downpipes held on by titanium studs. Through these pipes the V-twin uninhibitedly blasts out its hammering staccato for the benefit of the spectators at Ducati Club races.

27

The Verlicchi frame is largely standard but has been shorn of the lugs for the main stand and pillion seat. The Forcella-Italia fork has adjustable spring pre-load and damping, but the owner, who is a weight-fetishist (the Duke weighs only 334 lb or 152 kg), unscrewed the sliders, put in SAE 7 oil and gave them White Power fork springs. The alloy cantilever swinging arm with eccentric mountings comes from WBO, and was polished to a brilliant finish by Jörg Laibacher "in several night shifts. Yvonne served me Chianti and Parma ham while I worked away, and made it all quite bearable." Suspension and damping is taken care of by a White Power strut which, like the forks, has a multistage adjustment.

Marvic magnesium rims

custom biker. For the Battle of the Twins races, though, he might buy a standard Duke.

But only if Yvonne is still so understanding.

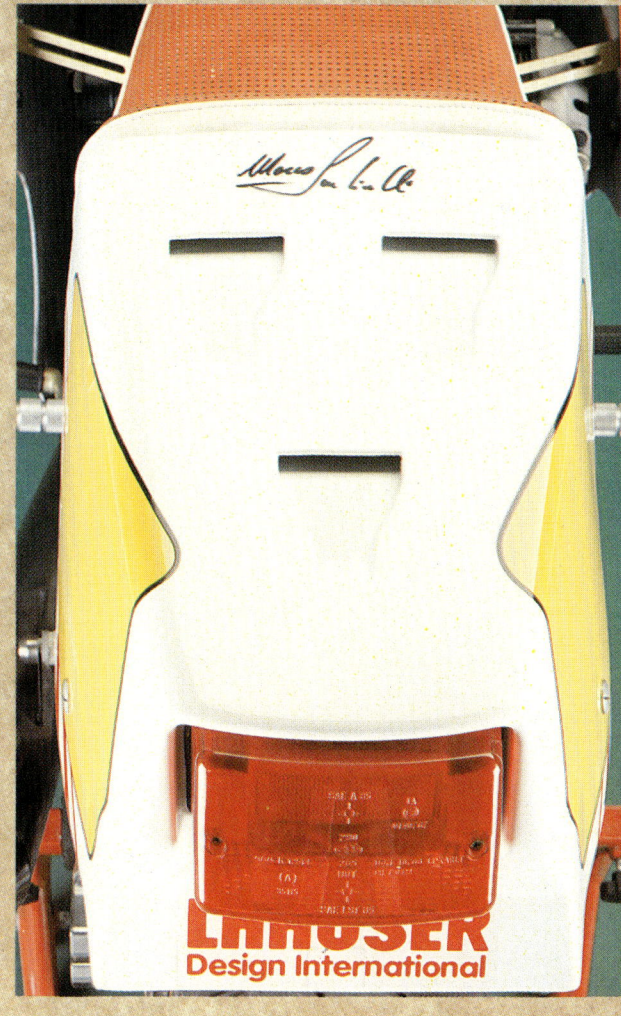

(3.50" x 17" front, 5.50" x 17" rear) with drilled-out spindles also help save weight. Safe braking is guaranteed by the Brembo floating twin disc system with 11-inch (280 mm) discs on the front wheel, even though Laibacher says that the P08 twin-piston calipers "aren't quite the business." A floating 10-inch (260 mm) Brembo disc brake helps keep down the unsprung weight on the rear wheel. Tank, saddle, and fairing are from the original Ducati F1, but a few details have been altered. The fairing, for instance, now has side air inlets and an enlarged opening for the oil cooler below the rectangular headlight. Laibacher's Ducati rebuild has cost him around $16,000. "For that I could have got an 851, but it would have been a standard model, and that's not what I wanted," says the

DATA SHEET

Engine	Air-cooled V-twin four-stroke
Bore & stroke	3.5 x 2.4 ins (88 x 61.5 mm)
Capacity	46 cu ins (749 cc)
Power	85 bhp at 9,000 rpm
Transmission	Five-speed gearbox
Wheelbase	57 ins (1440 mm)
Frame	Steel tubular lattice frame
Weight	334 lb (152 kg)
Maximum speed	131 mph (210 kph)
Production year	1985
Constructor	Jörg Laibacher/Ducati

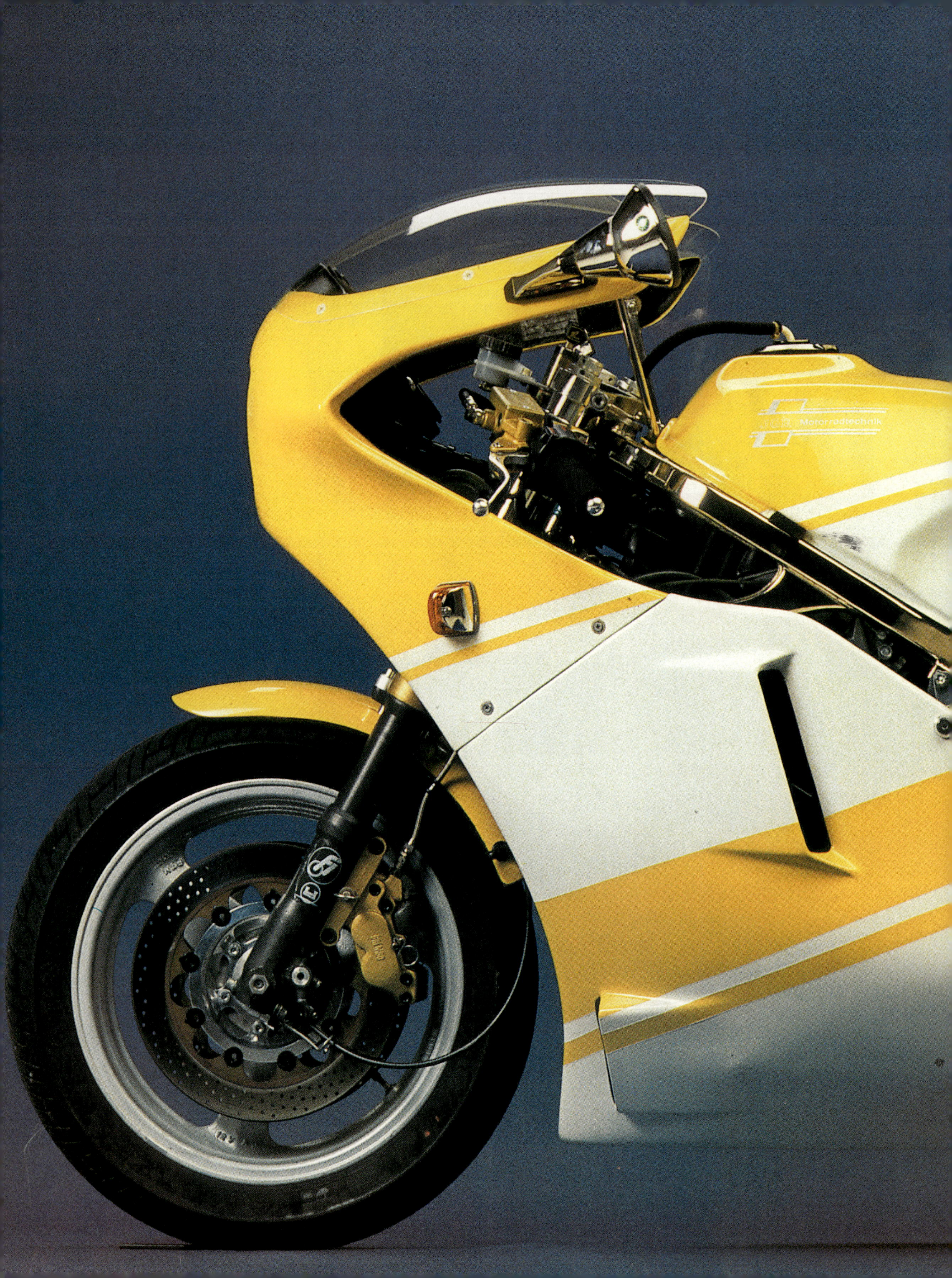
Motorradtechnik

Yellow Fever

For custom bikers, working on their machines is like a disease – and if you are also crazy about Honda V-4 engines and the color yellow, converting a VF 750F is the best cure.

You know the feeling. You are sitting alone at home, raindrops are hammering on the window, and all those gray clouds are getting you down. Yes, that's when the fever gets you. It's no use fighting it. Your actions become automatic, in fact they have a kind of ritual quality. You take your old Honda V-4 and dismantle everything, but everything, and begin to polish its frame with sandpaper and metal

32

33

polish. For days or even weeks, you fight the lonely battle of abrasive against pitted rust. At some point during one long night, you will at last be satisfied with your work and will give the frame to the specialist to be nickel-plated. But you can't get rid of the fever just like that, in fact only now does it really get a firm hold on you. You just have to make your Honda its own fairing, so a round lump takes shape in your hands. And however did you manage to burn around those corners with the standard brakes and fork? You've got to have an Italian racing kit, even if your bank manager starts to ask pointed questions. You just can't live without a Forcella-Italia 42 fork and Brembo Serie d'Oro brakes. But you still go hot and cold all over because you know that the engine needs yet more power. So you make a pilgrimage to the Honda tuning guru, Roland Eckert, and give him no peace until he hands over the HRC racing cams. And you will fit an RC-30 exhaust, although you know that it will still need extensive alterations.

If you get it really badly, you will end up painting the dials of the instruments yourself, having your initials engraved on the engine casing, increasing your loan to the equivalent of a year's salary, and buying nice wide wheels as well.

And then you will put the bike through the motor vehicle inspection, and having become your own manufacturer the fever will have gone down a little.

And then you'll have further ideas, because the rear swinging arm really ought to be polished too, and urgently.

DATA SHEET

Engine	Water-cooled V-four four-stroke
Bore & stroke	2.7 – 1.9 ins (70 – 48.6 mm)
Capacity	46 cu ins (748 cc)
Power	95 bhp at 10,500 rpm
Transmission	Five-speed gearbox
Wheelbase	58 ins (1480 mm)
Frame	Double cradle frame
Weight	506 lb (230 kg) with full tank
Maximum speed	142 mph (227 kph)
Production year	1987
Constructor	Jörgen Gaëbner/Honda

35

Simply Red

Simply red, but certainly not simple: Rödiger Flink's Egli Suzuki. Thanks to expert tuning, it's not only the power of the GSX-R 1100 which is just right.

FLINK

One day in the 80s, a Yamaha WS 750 found a new lord and master in Rüdiger Flink. Yet the relationship was not to last – the wildly weaving machine threw its rider out of the saddle after only a few miles at around 80 mph (130 kph). This was reason enough for Rüdiger Flink to look around for a new set of wheels. He eventually found what he was looking for in the stock of Fritz W. Egli, and ordered one of the precision-made Swiss frame kits. Gradually he completed it with the very finest components, and it became his dream Egli.

Power, power and more power was Flink's motto, so he decided on the Suzuki GSX-R 1100 engine as its source. However, even in the untamed version, the power was not enough for him. So he had the engine completely worked over in the LKM tuning shop. Wiseco pistons, increased compression, machined camshafts and open Mikuni slide carbs helped beef up the power unit, so that an impressive 160 bhp is available at the rear wheel. The exhaust gases from the Suzuki power unit are routed through a Schüle four-into-two-into-one system.

A White Power suspension unit at the rear and the renowned Egli forks in front, converted with precision

Teflon guides, ensure that the power of the red racer from the Rhineland is matched by excellent handling characteristics. 17-inch rims front and rear endow the rather unwieldy stock Egli with unaccustomed agility, and the four-piston Brembo racing brakes on the front wheel, together with the WiWo brake on the rear wheel, provide effective stopping power. The Egli's maximum speed is well up there in the superbike range: 180 mph (290 kph), it is claimed – extraordinarily impressive for any road bike, and a figure which puts the Flink Suzuki in the same league as fully fledged racing machines. The maximum speed also reflects the aerodynamic qualities of this well-designed machine. The bright red streamlined fairing and the seat are supplied by Speer, and give the Flink-

Egli a very special aura. True perfection, however, is revealed only when the fairing is removed.

A meticulously installed custom-made electrical system, titanium engine brackets and color-anodized turned aluminum parts prove that esthetics and functionality were no mere superficial concepts for Rüdiger Flink, but were the guiding principles behind the construction of the machine. Perfection is also written large in the finish of the frame and wheels chosen for this high-class machine: a plastic coating (in classic red, naturally) gives corrosion no chance.

Flink does not believe he can make many more improvements to his "red hot bike" for the moment: "452 lb (205 kg) with a full tank is about as far as you can go," he says, "and anyway, after three years in the making, it's about time to do some hard riding and burn some rubber!"

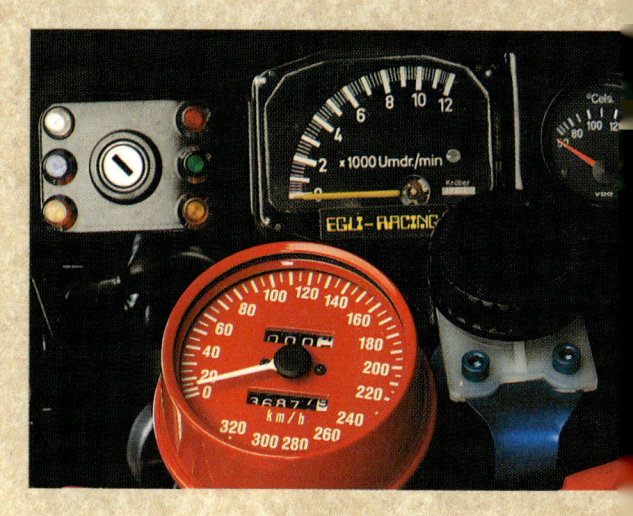

DATA SHEET

Engine	In-line four-cylinder four-stroke air/oil-cooled
Bore & stroke	3.0 x 2.3 ins (78 x 59 mm)
Capacity	69 cu ins (1127 cc)
Power	160 bhp at 10,800 rpm
Transmission	Five-speed gearbox
Wheelbase	59 ins (1500 mm)
Frame	Center tube steel frame
Weight	452 lb (205 kg) with full tank
Maximum speed	180 mph (290 kph)
Production year	1990
Constructor	Rödiger Flink/Egli

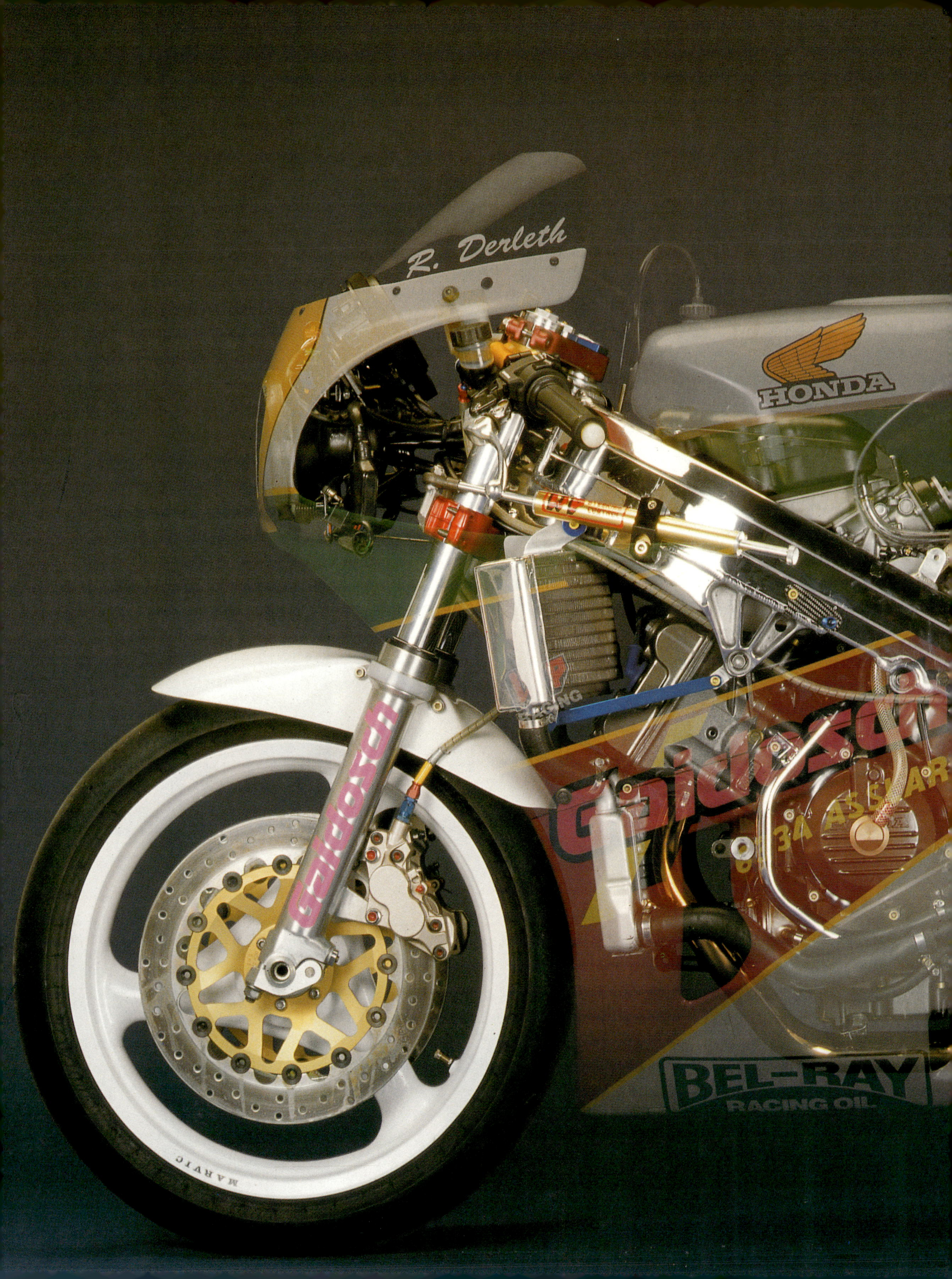
R. Derleth
HONDA
Gaidosch
Gaidosch
BEL-RAY
RACING OIL

Gear teeth

When dental technician Rainer Derleth is fed up with dentures, he can still give a snappy performance on the race circuit.

We all have a little of the urge to race in our blood. But one man whose veins are simply bursting with it is Rainer Derleth. This self-employed 35-year-old spends almost every spare minute on one racetrack or another with his Honda RC 30. If you watch him ride you'll soon notice that he's no beginner. His personal best time of 8 minutes, 42 seconds for the Nordschleife (the original long circuit at the Nürburgring) is proof of that.

If we take a look at his RC 30, we find one technical treat after another. He had to have something special, not a standard model. And it had to be a racer, but a street-legal one to be eligible for the Zuvi races for roadgoing machines. So a once-standard RC 30 turned into a superbike with full approval from the testing authorities. The engine alone is sheer perfection — he had it brought right up to racing pitch by Honda tuner Roland Gaidosch, with HRC pistons, increased compression, and a modified exhaust system. The V4 gives a stupendous 124 bhp in its easy-on-the-ear roadgoing trim. For

44

45

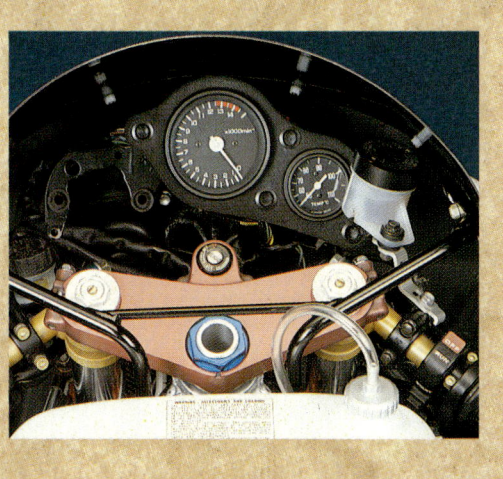

the running gear too only the finest components were used. The White Power swinging arm, for instance, was made specially for this machine, and was personally set up by WP boss Benny Wilbers. Almost as a matter of course the fairing and its fixtures are made of outrageously expensive super-light Kevlar/carbon fiber laminate. The formula for boosting performance: save weight. So it's no surprise that this expensive package is held together by a good number of nuts and bolts in top-strength aluminum alloy, or even precious titanium. But functional perfection alone was not enough for our fast-moving dental technician; the looks had to be just right to set it off. The frame and swinging arm were stripped of their paint and, after many hard-working sessions in the workshop, polished to such a high shine that in bright sunlight the wearing of welder's goggles is recommended. So that the dazzle doesn't get too extreme, all remaining alloy parts were coated with colored Eloxal. A superlative paint job dispels any last doubt as to the quality of the

DATA SHEET

Engine	Water-cooled V-four four-stroke
Bore & stroke	2.7 x 1.9 ins (70 x 48.6 mm)
Capacity	46 cu ins (748 cc)
Power	126 bhp at 12,000 rpm
Transmission	Six-speed gearbox
Wheelbase	55 ins (1410 mm)
Frame	Alloy tubular bridge frame
Weight	429 lb (195 kg) with full tank
Maximum speed	156 mph (250 kph)
Production year	1990
Constructor	Rainer Derleth/Bernhard Gaidosch /Honda

Derleth Honda. Anyone who suspects that our custom biker rides his lightweight circuit-going projectile – 429 lb (195 kg) with a full tank – at all circumspectly, for fear of wrecking it, can be reassured: "I didn't build it for the living room, I built it for the racetrack, and it's only really at home there." He's right, and we hope that our dental technician does just as neat a job on his customers' teeth as he did on his dream bike.

47

Perfectionism

A home-built three-in-line 500? That's no problem for Dieter Klopfer. His custom racing machine impresses by the perfectionism evident in its technical solutions, down to the smallest detail.

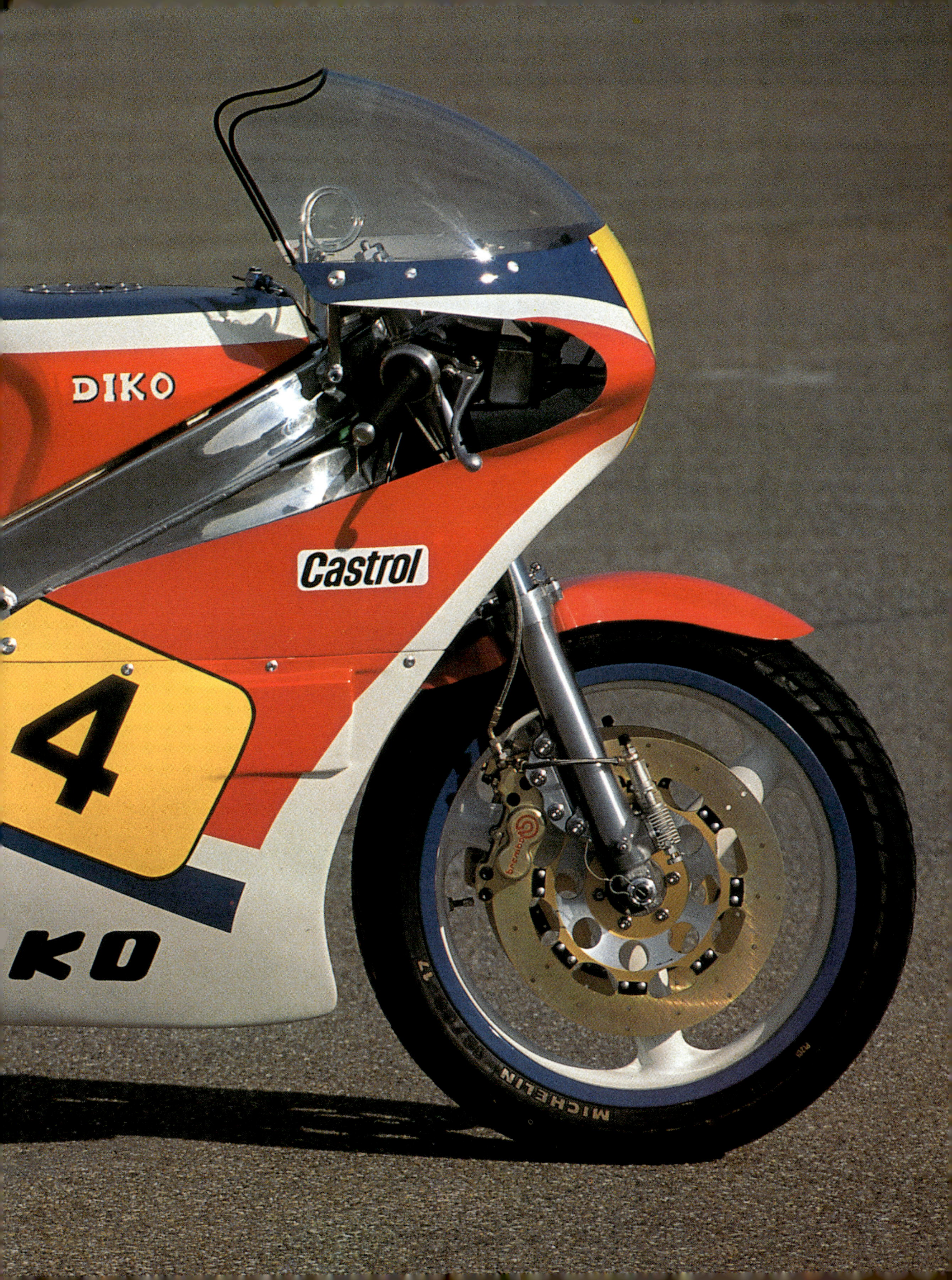
DIKO
Castrol
4
KO
MICHELIN

Perfectionism means fixing the fuel tank breather, not with adhesive tape, but with a wire through the fairing panel. Perfectionism means machining your water pump out of solid metal, driving it with a toothed belt, and matching the output of the pump to the length of the race by using different gearing. Perfectionism means fixing the expansion chamber to the exhaust pipe, not with a simple jubilee clip or springs, but by cutting a fine thread on the pipe and the pot and screwing them together. And perfectionism means stopping the swinging arm nut from coming loose, not by means of a shoddy bent over washer, but by placing a plastic wedge against the flats of the nut and screwing it down with a grubscrew. Or is this all a bit over the top?

You see, in these pages we have for your delectation something very special. It is one of the most beautiful and most perfect self-built machines we have ever seen. Anyone who has ever had any feeling for precision craftsmanship, anyone who has ever felt inwardly that the seemingly impossible can be done, will be really enthusiastic about this 500. For each part of the Diko 500 has had unimaginable trouble lavished on it. It is only logical that such a work of art could not be created in the space of a year. No, several man-years were needed for this, man-years of meticulous detail work.

We were all the more astonished, then, to hear that for 10 years Dieter Klopfer has subjected his machine to the severe stresses of racing, and that it will continue to go into action on the racing circuits of Europe. From time to time its builder and inventor just has to get a proper whiff of the racetrack in his nostrils.

But let's look at the bike. You have probably realized that this is a three-cylinder machine, from the three exhaust pipes. But a three-in-line 500 — was such a thing ever made? No, so it must be a self-built machine then. Correct — Klopfer got the idea for such a motor in 1979, when he first saw a three-cylinder engine of this kind, based on the reliable Yamaha TZ 350, in a sidecar combination. But instead of simply welding together two crankcases, Klopfer machined one for the third cylinder out of solid metal, and bolted it on to the original case. With the cylinders, he had no other choice but to weld together two cut-up Yamaha TZ blocks, because these are made in one piece. He cut off half a cylinder from each one, and welded together the resulting one-and-a-half cylinder blocks; bore them out, hone them, and there's your three-cylinder block. Arch-do-it-yourselfer Klopfer then fitted the three separate water jackets and made a one-piece cylinder head, complete with coolant channels, out of solid metal. Transmission shafts were also made by his skilled hand; the layshaft has to be longer than usual, since the engine is offset to the right. He even made the gear wheels himself, in order to accommodate his particular requirements as to gear ratios. The clutch, with its beautifully drilled and lightened housing, is also a custom-made part.

All Klopfer's creative energies were employed on the exhaust system. Countless metal sheets had to be beaten and bent into the correct shape. Any ordinary mortal has

51

enough trouble in making anything better than a crooked tin can. Klopfer seems to be a master of the art of metalworking. We can well imagine all the cutting, bending, and beating of the individual sheets that was necessary before they were welded to form the elegantly curved silencers. And then a screw-on rear expansion chamber – what absolute madness! On the intake side, three 1.4 inch (35 mm) piston slide Mikuni carburetors with beautifully rounded venturis provide the mixture; their throttle cables slide in alloy outer tubes.

Dieter Klopfer tuned his engine over many hours of test-bed running. As the reward for his trouble, the indicator needle recorded a healthy 117 bhp at 13,000 rpm. A lot for a three-cylinder engine, especially one which gets by with a simple set of ports, having no inlet or exhaust valve system to boost its performance. Enough in any case to win two titles in the German hill-climbing contests, and numerous notable placings among the first five 500s in the German championship.

At that time, however, the three-cylinder had to perform in an Egli frame. For the 1990 season Dieter Klopfer prescribed a drastic remedy for his Diko's handling. As always, he did a very thorough job, and sent his engine off to the renowned frame-builder, Spondon, in England. The top-notch British tubesmith, enthused by the splendid engine, bent up an equally magnificent frame around the motor. The tubes curve around the cylinder block in a marvellously logical and sympathetic way, and add to its compactness the eye-catching attractions of polished alloy. An elderly and therefore very

To be consistent, only the very finest parts were good enough when it came to the brakes. Zanzani discs, made in very small numbers, were exactly what was wanted. Their floating mounting consists of two locating sleeves held between steel retaining plates. A costly solution, but in the end just right for the Diko. That the fairing, tank, and seat hump are not bought in, but rather are Klopfer's own handiwork, should come as no surprise to us. The stylish fairing grew out of a Honda top half and a Suzuki bottom half. The individual parts had, of course, to be painstakingly altered until they blended into such a harmonious whole. The best glass fiber laminate was used for the seat hump; both this and the fairing are extremely light, as is of course the home-welded alloy tank.

Granted, the development of racing machines has proceeded apace since the three-cylinder Diko was conceived, which embodies the spirit of the late 70s and early 80s. For all of that, though, the Diko is far from ready for the scrapheap, as future race results will doubtless prove — and it will be the triumph of perfectionism.

experienced English gentleman must have plied the welding rod and inert gas here with a marvellously steady hand; each drop of weld-metal follows the next so precisely. Ordinary mortals can only dream of ever making such a weld — and above all, one which will hold. Years of experience and love of the material are needed, such as are still found, thank goodness, in the dusty old workshops of some British welders. The frame tubes had to be set up asymmetrically so as not to cramp the left-hand cylinder and its carburetor too much.

DATA SHEET

Engine	Water-cooled in-line three-cylinder two-stroke
Bore & stroke	2.5 x 2 ins (64 x 51.8 mm)
Capacity	30 cu ins (498 cc)
Power	117 bhp at 13,000 rpm
Transmission	Six-speed gearbox
Wheelbase	53 ins (1340 mm)
Frame	Alloy tubular bridge frame
Weight	308 lb (140 kg) with full tank
Maximum speed	191 mph (305 kph)(on the Avus banked track)
Production year	1983
Constructor	Dieter Klopfer

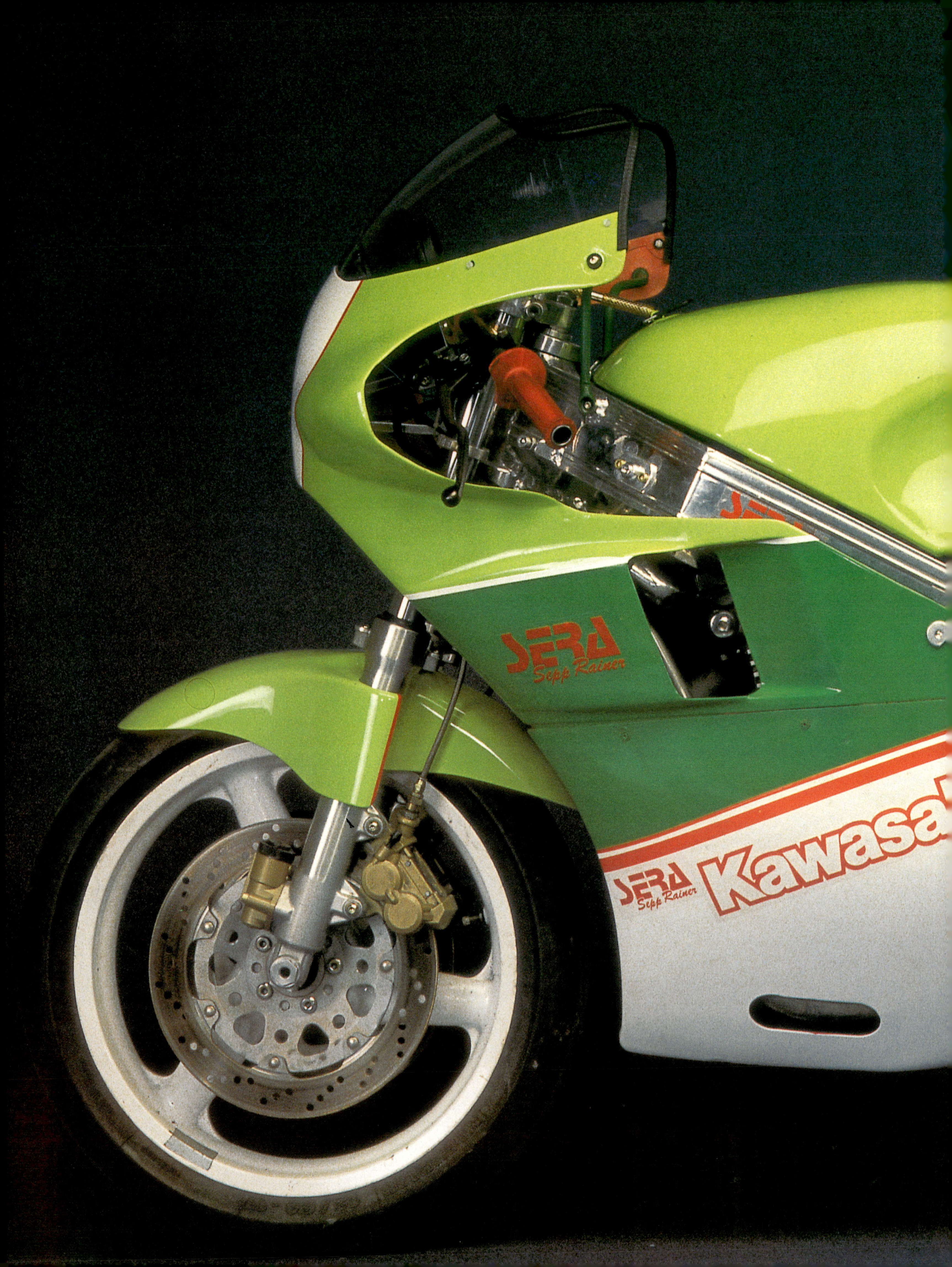
SERA
Sepp Rainer
SERA
Sepp Rainer
Kawasa

Light and wild

Sepp Rainer's custom-built machine with the Kawasaki GPZ 500S engine raises the old question of whether lightweight construction or power output is more important.

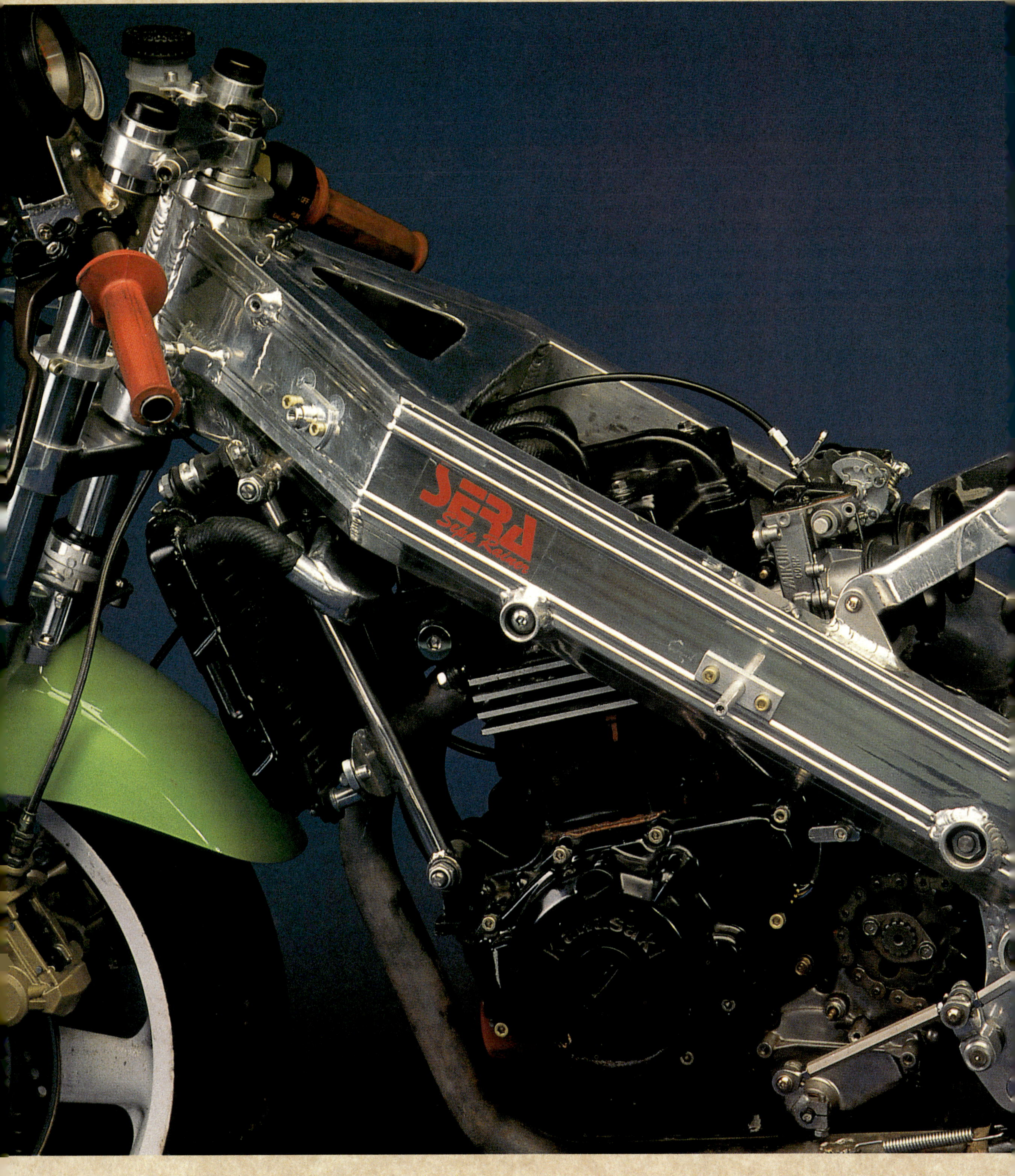
SERA

Sepp Rainer, whose initials SERA already adorn many a frame, had an idea: Why do racers in the German Battle of the Twins championship always have to steam along using a hefty 61 cu ins (1000 cc) engine; a small, light twin could do the work just as well. The Kawasaki GPZ 500S, already endowed with an amazing 60 bhp ex-works, provided him with the right power unit. Around it he tailored an aluminum frame whose quality of craftsmanship bears comparison with the best products of professional European tuners.

The direct connection of the steering head with the swinging arm bearing by means of thin-walled, large-section aluminum extrusions promises strength with low weight, as does the generously proportioned swinging arm. White Power telescopic arms and a Suzuki GSX-R fork provide a convincing solution to the suspension problem.

In order to beef up the Kawasaki twin engine a little, increasing the swept volume was the obvious way to go. The cylinder block was bored out by an amazing 0.355 inches (9 mm), so that pistons from a Wiseco Yamaha FJ 1100 rebore kit could be fitted. This was the absolute maximum, as the present 0.315 inch (8 mm) wall thickness between the cylinders is already on the limit of what is possible. Because of this, problems arose at the beginning of road testing with the fragile cylinder head gasket, but these were solved by using copper.

Otto Geppert from Kappeln reworked the piston to suit the Kawasaki cylinder head, and in so doing raised the compression ratio to 12.5:1. He also lightened the crank assembly by 5.5 lb (2.5 kg). Inlet valves a quarter of an inch (4 mm) larger than usual, and exhaust valves an eighth of an inch (2 mm) larger speed up gas-flow, as do the 1.5 inch (38 mm) Mikuni slide-valve carburetors. The exhaust system is one of Sera's own products, but is certainly not the last word in sophis-

rpm on gives useful power. Then from 8,000 you get the real push, and a loud roar from the exhaust pipes accompanies the power bulge. It is amazing how smoothly the engine runs, in spite of the big pistons and the radically pared-down balancing shaft.

tication; similarly the valves are still operated by standard cams. The thermal well-being of the twin, now grown to 39 cu ins (643 cc), is taken care of by a Citroen 2CV oil-cooler. In this state the engine yields a genuine 75 bhp. We had the opportunity of riding the Sera-Kawa on the Hockenheim circuit. The twin ticks over smoothly, and from 4,000

DATA SHEET

Engine	Water-cooled twin-cylinder four-stroke
Bore & stroke	3.2 x 2.3 ins (83 x 58 mm)
Capacity	39 cu ins (643 cc)
Power	75 bhp at 11,000 rpm
Transmission	Six-speed gearbox
Wheelbase	53 ins (1345 mm)
Frame	Aluminum tubular bridge frame
Weight	308 lb (140 kg) with full tank
Maximum speed	150 mph (240 kph)
Production year	1989
Constructor	Sepp Rainer/Kawasaki

Star Performer

A ride on Heiko Heinemeyer's Kawasaki Z 550 is pure heaven for addicts of high-revs: only at 12,800 rpm does the twin-valve Kawasaki go into orbit with its 92 bhp.

We sit down on the foam rubber-padded seat, and concentrate. A gentle twist of the grip on the right-hand handlebar end, and the tachometer needle flashes round the dial: 8,000, 9,000, 11,000 – just don't let it fall below 8,000, or the four-cylinder motor dies as soon as you let the clutch in.

Through the two-stroke smoke of the blaring Suzuki RGVs and Yamaha RD 350s all around (along with a few Honda VF 500s and Kawasaki ZXR 400s) we vaguely glimpse the starting-light: green – and they're off, these lawn-mowers with their standard low-ratio gears. By contrast, the six-speed racing gearbox of our Heinemeyer Z 550 goes up to 75 mph in first. But a Moto-Aktiv four-hour race is not decided in the first lap, and the Zeltweg circuit is, after all, no go-kart track. Anyhow, 92 bhp at 12,800 rpm is good for around 145 mph (230 kph) on the fastest stretches. Our Bakker tubular lattice frame gives exemplary handling; no

62

putting the lights into place and sorting out the background – we're in the pit lane in Zeltweg. Slightly irritated, we get off the Kawasaki and turn to Heiko Heinemeyer who is standing in the background and smiling.

"Basically, it's a 1979 Z 500. I bought the Bakker frame in 1986, and three years later the machine passed its motor vehicle inspection; it had double-spoked wheels, a twin-leading-shoe drum brake in front, and a half-fairing. Since 1990 the machine has looked as it does now, and it has also run in races in this form."

wonder, with a wheelbase of just 53.5 inches (1360 mm) and a 4-inch trail. And a mere 328 lb (149 kg) with a full tank should also mean that, weighing next to nothing, it stops well. The 11-inch twin discs in front do in fact give really powerful braking. But then they come from the 1990 Suzuki RGV 250, a favorite source of parts for Heiko Heinemeyer: fairing, 17-inch wheels, brakes, and forks are all borrowed from the little two-stroke and adapted for his custom racer.

"Now can we at last make a start with the photos?" says a grouchy voice. The voice belongs to photographer Frank Herzog, who is just

63

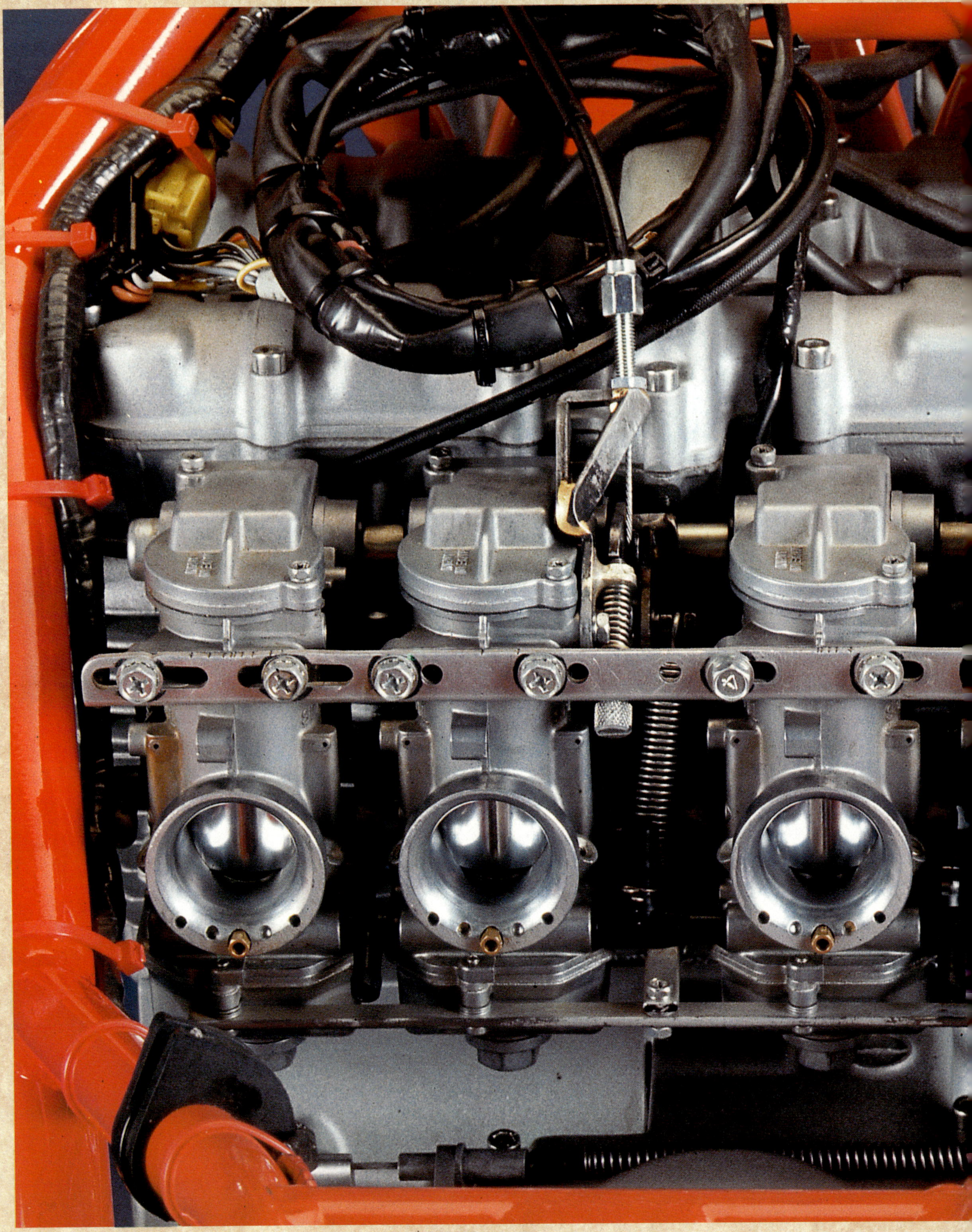

The outstanding feature is however the old Kawasaki twin-valve 500 engine, a copy of the erstwhile Honda CB 500 four right down to the bottom of its sump. The Z 400 crankshaft plus a stroke of only 1.8 inches (47 mm) and a bore of 2.4 inches (61 mm) make for an unburstable 33.5 cu in (549 cc) engine. Camshafts profiled by the owner to give extreme timing push against 1.3 inch (33 mm) inlet and 1.1 inch (29 mm) exhaust valves. Keikin CR 33 racing carburetors send a high-octane mixture to the cylinders, which have a high (11.5:1) compression ratio. Forged Mahle pistons cope with the increased combustion pressure. It goes without saying that all superfluous ancillary units and engine covers have been dispensed with.

"Of course it was insane to go to all that trouble, but I simply had to know what could be done with the engine," says Heiko. How long does it last? "You strip it down after every race to check it. There's an oil temperature of 150° in the sump: the valves and pistons don't really like that in the long run. That's why I'm not racing any more – not on this one." On which one, then? The answer: Heiko Heinemeyer is working on a single-cylinder machine for the SoS (Sound of Singles) races.

DATA SHEET

Engine	Air-cooled four-cylinder in-line four-stroke
Bore & stroke	2.4 x 1.8 ins (61 x 47 mm)
Capacity	33 cu ins (549 cc)
Power	92 bhp at 12,800 rpm
Transmission	Six-speed gearbox
Wheelbase	53.5 ins (1360 mm)
Frame	Steel tubular lattice frame
Weight	328 lb (149 kg) with full tank
Maximum speed	147 mph (235 kph)
Production year	1986, rebuilt 1990
Constructors	Heiko Heinemeyer/Nicco Bakker/Kawasaki

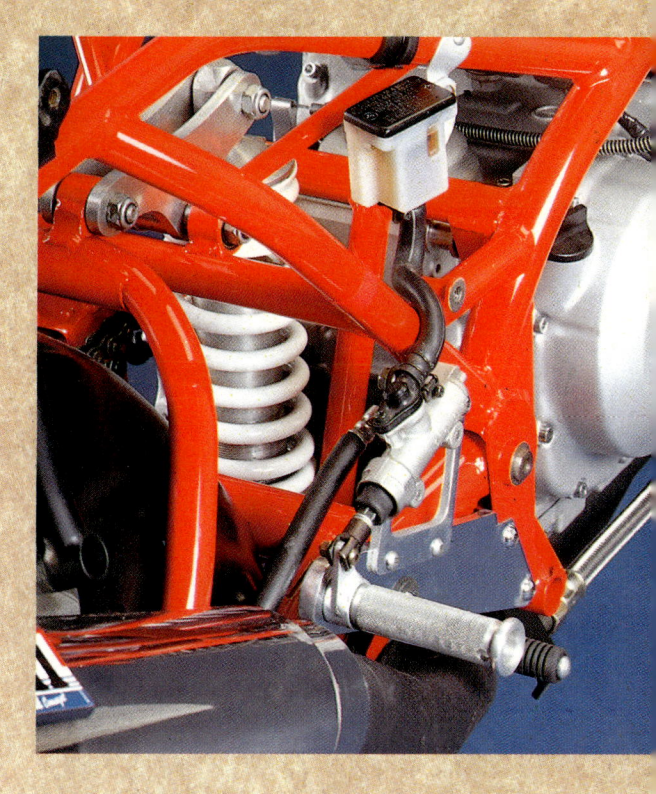

Eifel Power

Three men from the Eifel had always been interested in powerful singles. The result of their enthusiasm is a racing machine with the large-capacity single cylinder of a Suzuki DR Big.

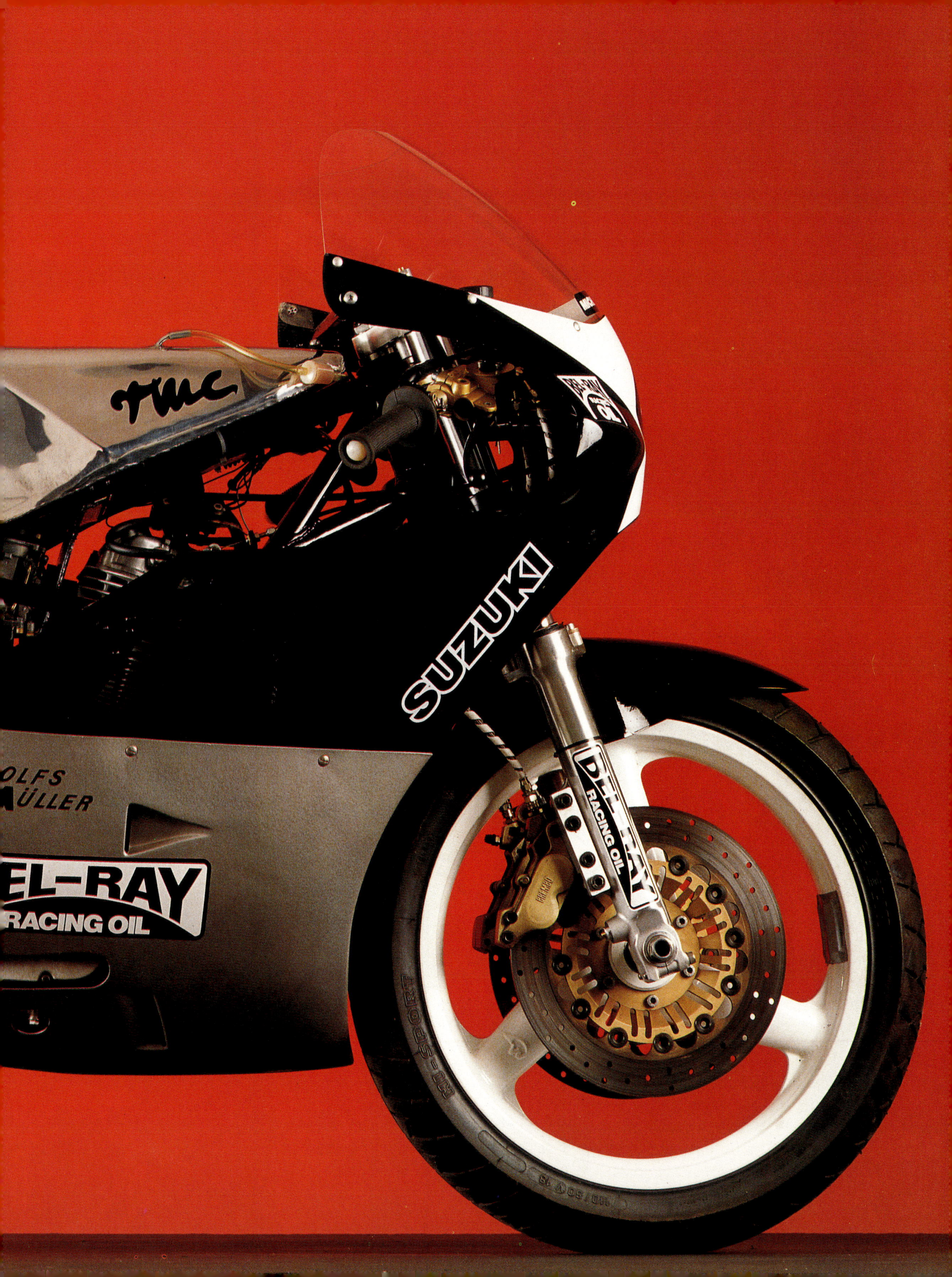
SUZUKI
RACING OIL

S ome people are simply obsessive. A dream lurks in their minds, gives them sleepless nights, and turns them into bundles of nerves. In the case of Peter Müller, Horst Rolfs, and Gerd Clemens they were dreaming of a motorbike. Not any old bike, of course. After all, the Rolfs-Müller duo owns a Suzuki dealership. No, it had to be something

68

special. A custom-built machine, in fact. It had to be a large-capacity four-stroke single with raceworthy running gear, for the Sound of Singles races. No sooner said than done. The

69

basic formula is simple: dig out from the murky depths of the spare parts store a DR Big engine and a large quantity of GSX-R parts. Then shut yourself in a quiet room and design a tubular lattice frame. The hefty 46 cu in (750 cc) engine is built into this as part of the structure. The frame specification should be the same as for the GSX-R 750. To this are added as many standard parts from the 750 super sports bike as possible, such as a swinging arm, forks, and

70

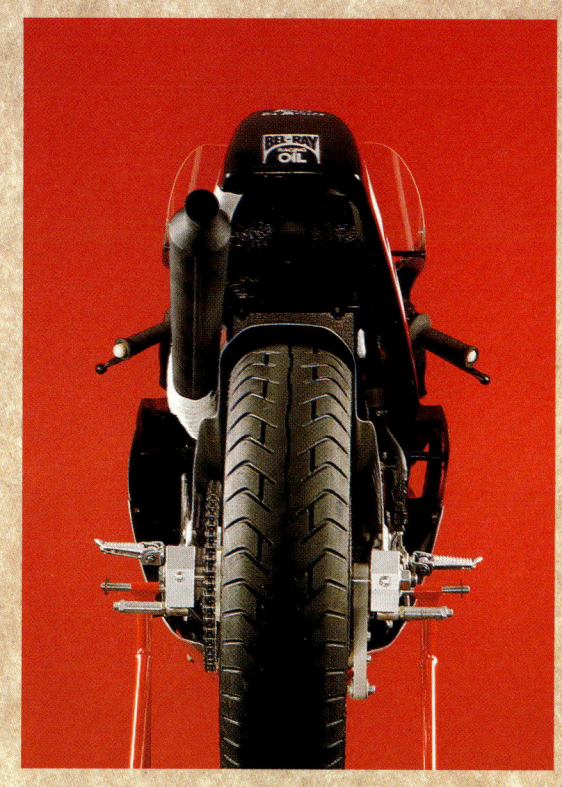

suspension struts. Finally the project is completed with such ingredients as Brembo brakes, Marvic rims and a Honda RS 250 fairing. For about three months the trio spent every available minute in the workshop in order to make their dream come true. And in its first race outing Peter Müller immediately took seventh place.

DATA SHEET

Engine	Air- and oil-cooled single cylinder four-stroke
Bore & stroke	4 x 3.3 ins (105 x 84 mm)
Capacity	44 cu ins (727 cc)
Power	55 bhp at 7,500 rpm
Transmission	Five-speed gearbox
Wheelbase	55.5 ins (1410 mm)
Frame	Steel tubular lattice frame
Weight	308 lb (140 kg) with full tank
Maximum speed	130 mph (208 kph)
Production year	1989
Constructors	Horst Rolfs/Peter Müller/Gerd Clemens/Suzuki

71

Single-Bells

Oh what fun it is to ride, on a one-lung motorbike.... This fabulous racing single carries a bored-out Yamaha single-cylinder engine in its Egli frame. The other ingredients, too, are of the finest quality.

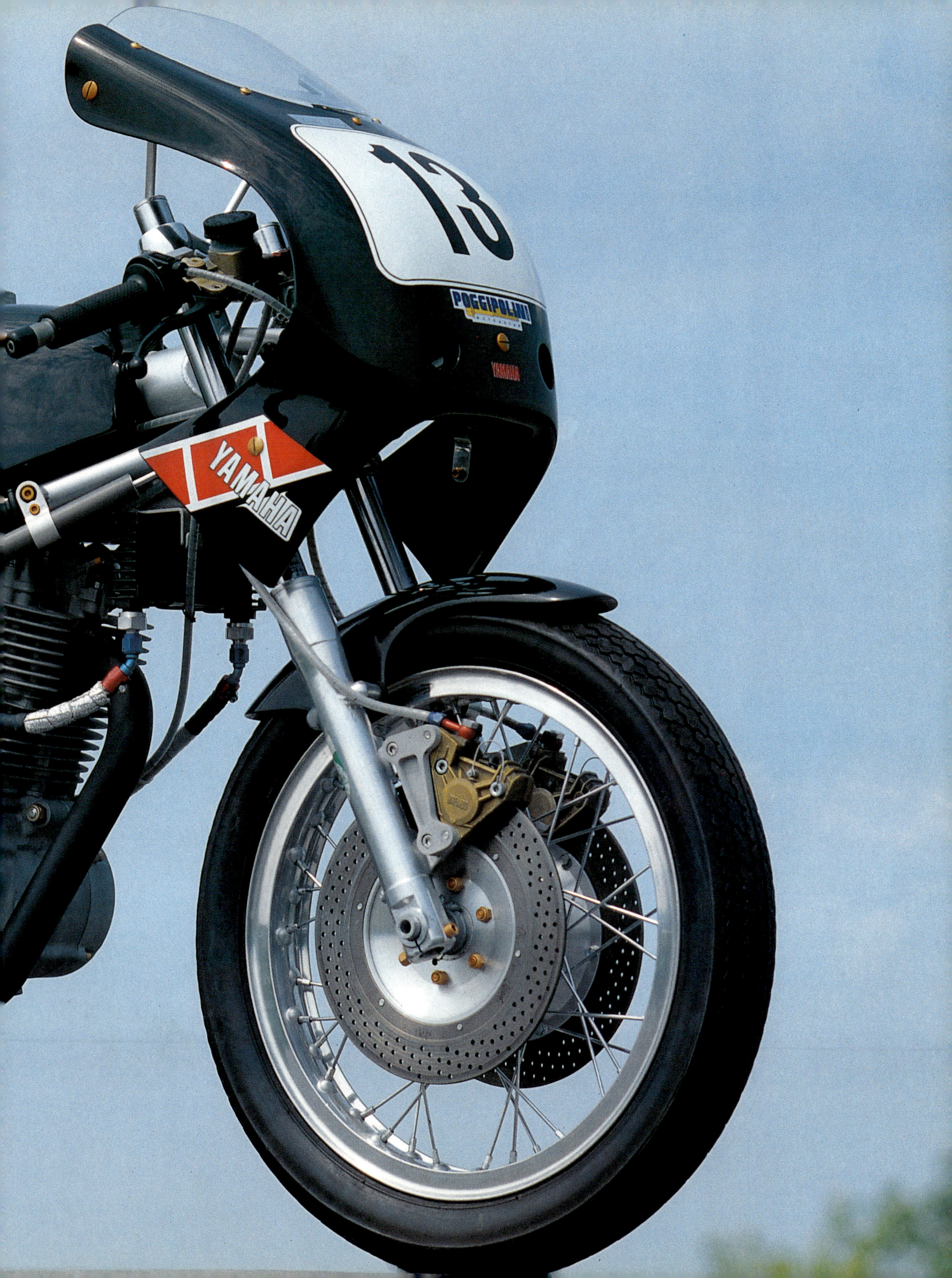
13
POGGIPOLINI
YAMAHA
YAMAHA

Originally, Peter Luscher from Salzburg built this racer for a friend, who suddenly decided to have nothing more to do with motorbikes. So our Austrian simply added the dark beauty to his stable of Ducatis, a black sheep, so to speak, amidst all his thoroughbred red Italian steeds. But in the SoS (Sound of Singles) races so far, this custom bike has turned out to be more like a wolf in sheep's clothing. "In practice at Zeltweg last year we had earned ourselves third place on the starting grid, but because the big-end bearing was done for, the engine vibrated so fiercely that we didn't even get to start." "We" are Peter Luscher from Salzburg, the builder of the Yamaha-Egli hybrid, and Robert Fischinger, who rides the machine in the races.

74

The heart of the Luscher Yamaha is a TT 500 engine, bored out to 33 cu ins (540 cc) and tuned up using all the tricks of the trade: modified lubrication system with an oil-cooler, 1.7 inch (42.5 mm) choke Dell'Orto carburetors with dedicated cooling,

75

widened intake and exhaust tracts with larger valves, a hotter camshaft, and lightened rocker-arms. The crankshaft carries a machined H-section connecting rod, crowned by a 3.6 inch (92 mm) Mahle piston.

This work of art sits in an Egli frame; the swinging arm comes from Franz Brandauer, who was also responsible for the alloy frames of Freddy Spencer's racers. The other items of running gear come from Italy: Marzocchi forks and telescopic arms, Borrani high-profile rims, and Campagnolo hubs. The Brembo brake calipers, on the other hand, act on custom-made discs.

Alloy tank, fairing, and seat were made in Peter Luscher's workshop. For his high-quality custom bikes he uses almost exclusively ultra-light and correspondingly expensive Poggipolini bolts in titanium or Ergol alloy. All this costs a lot of money, of course, but Luscher aims for the highest possible degree of perfection and cost is no object. One look at this custom bike tells you that.

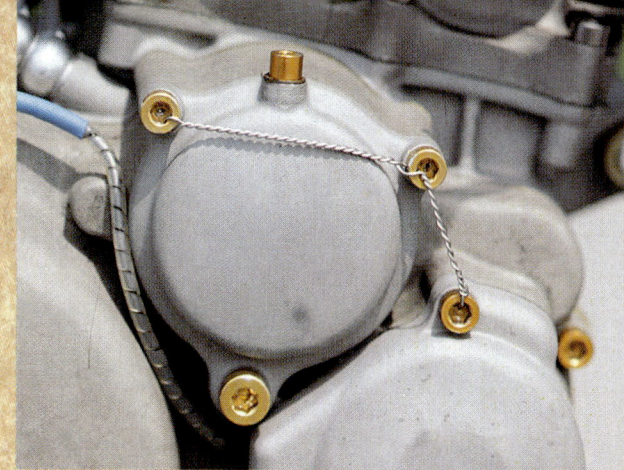

DATA SHEET

Engine	Air-cooled single cylinder four-stroke
Bore & stroke	3.6 x 3.2 ins (92 x 81 mm)
Capacity	33 cu ins (540 cc)
Power	40 bhp at 7,000 rpm
Transmission	Five-speed gearbox
Wheelbase	53.5 ins (1360 mm)
Frame	Steel center spine frame
Weight	308 lb (140 kg) with full tank
Maximum speed	112 mph (180 kph)
Production year	1989
Constructor	Peter Luscher/Yamaha

Mad in Germany

Anyone who enters a Harley-Davidson in the German BoT class for big twins must be a little crazy. But that doesn't worry one Harley dealer – he took his heavy metal machine to the racetrack to prove something.

TREUSCH
MOTORRAD RENNSPORT PARTS
TEL. 0621/477243

Still the Greatest

You have to be a little crazy to enter the German Battle of the Twins Championship with a Harley. Hans Bernhard, an independent Harley-Davidson dealer, and rider Gerhard Treusch have done just this. The machine on the starting line for the first round of the BoT championship in Speyer is the result of an idea which came up one beery evening in the fall of 1987 in Frankenthal. "The machines you see in this class in the USA have fascinated us for a long time," says Bernhard. "We don't reckon we have any great chance of success, but a Harley in the field does add to the interest."

They would certainly win the prize for the most noise, since what leaves the combustion chambers of the cast

80

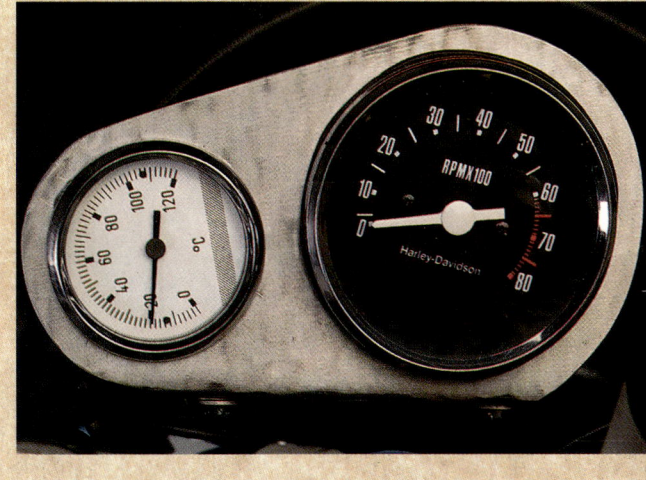

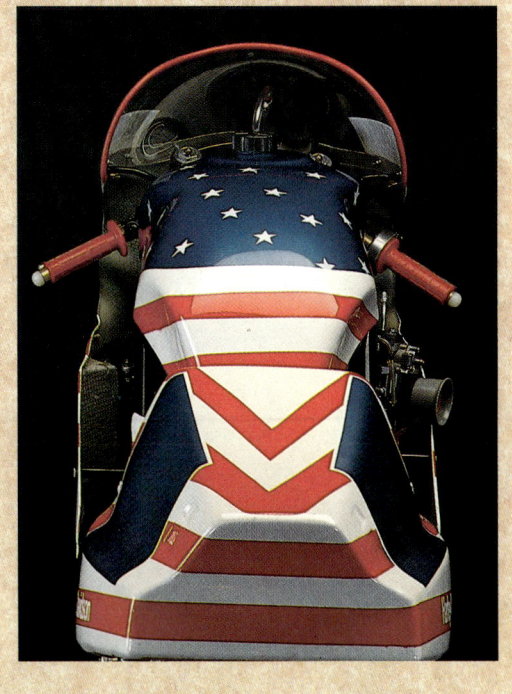

iron cylinders via the stainless steel exhaust is reminiscent of a heavy metal band really belting it out. The XR 1000 engine was the basis of the power unit, with Andrews cams, semi-electronic Accel ignition, lighter pushrods, 3.2 x 3.8 in (81 x 96 mm) bore and stroke, a higher compression ratio and 1.6 inch (40 mm) Mikuni carburetors. Bernhard promises 100 bhp at 5,800 rpm; even 90 would be achievement enough. Four gears suffice, as first has a very high ratio. The tubular lattice frame is supplied by Buell, the American tuning specialist, while the Marzocchi M1 R forks are a high-grade Italian addition. In front Buell double-piston calipers with 13-inch (320 mm) Spondon discs, and at the back Grimeca brakes provide the retardation. The wheels are 17-inch Dymax, 3.5 front and 5.5 rear, equipped with Michelin radials.

Treusch made the tank and fairing components out of extremely light kevlar; the tank weighs 2.2 lb (1 kg). The figures resulting from this light-weight construction are impressive: a mere 397 lb with battery and fuel — not bad with this massive iron lump of an engine. Bernhard has invested between $23,000 and $29,000 in the project.

DATA SHEET

Engine	Air-cooled V-twin four-stroke
Bore & stroke	3.2 x 3.8 ins (81 x 96 mm)
Capacity	61 cu ins (998 cc)
Power	100 bhp at 5,800 rpm
Transmission	Five-speed gearbox
Wheelbase	59 ins (1490 mm)
Frame	Steel tubular lattice frame
Weight	397 lb (180 kg) with full tank
Maximum speed	up to 155 mph (250 kph), depending on gearing
Production year	1987
Constructor	Hans Bernhard/Harley

No objection, Your Honor

After 1,500 hours a lawyer had successfully brought to completion his most difficult brief: an entirely custom-built project, complete with self-built engine.

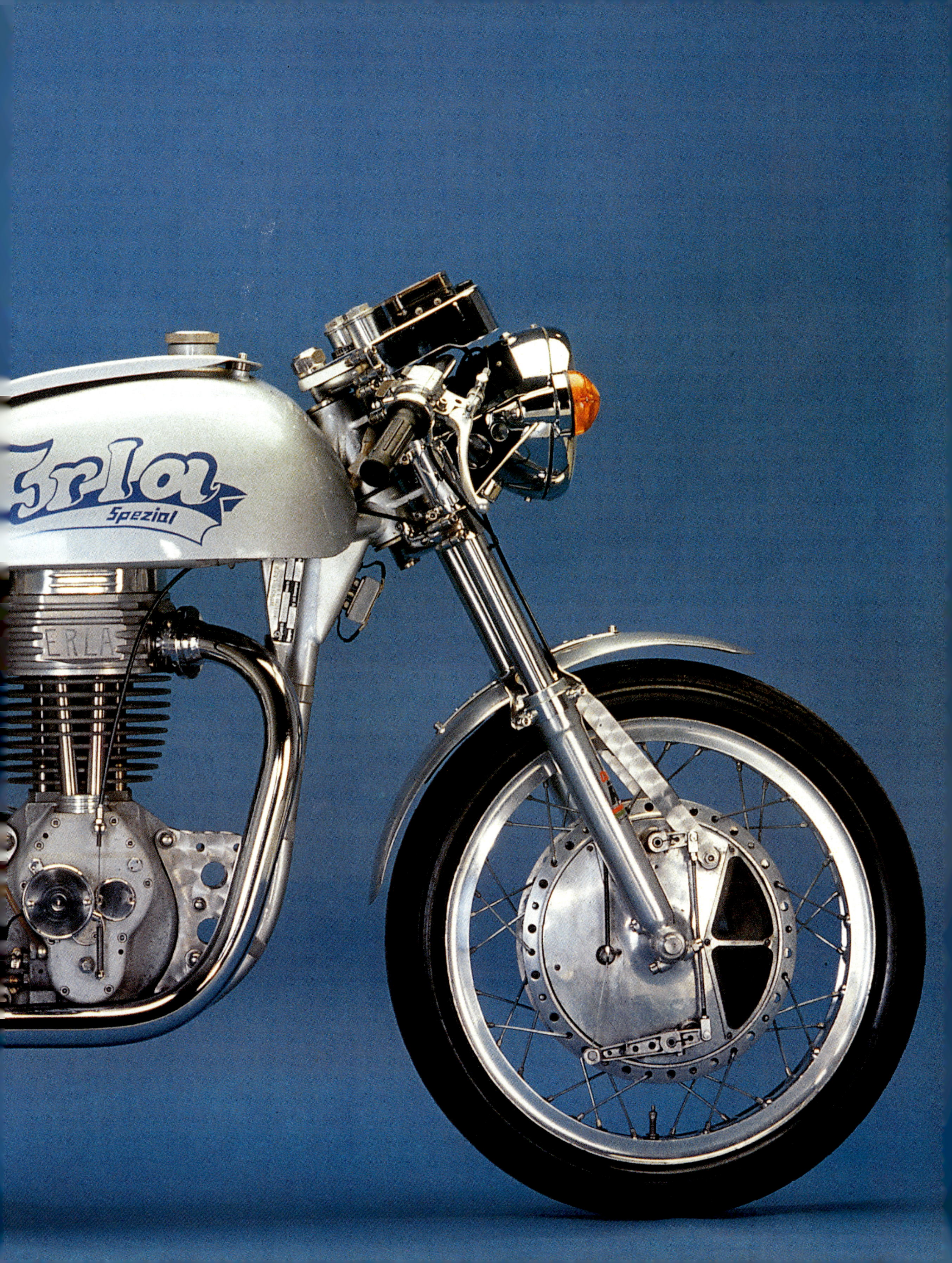
Erla
Spezial
ERLA

It was all the fault of the famous JAP engines. The year was 1955, and these British power units dominated the sport of dirt-track racing. Erich Lawrenz was fascinated by them and began to ride in races himself. Since then the lawyer has spent every free minute in his small workshop. The time came when Lawrenz could no longer resist the urge: a self-built motorcycle with a single-cylinder pushrod engine entirely of his own construction would really be something. Ideas became drawings, drawings became models, and after a total of 1,500

87

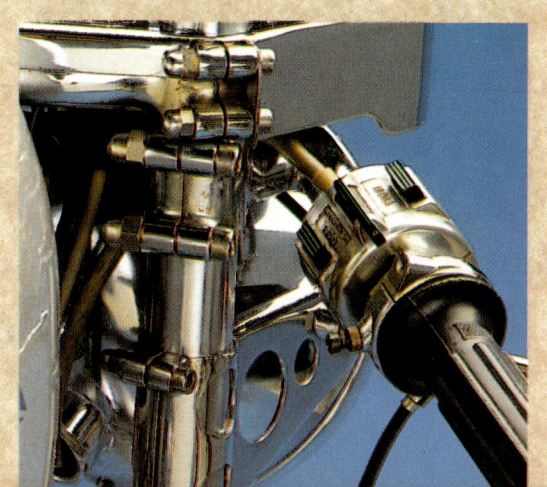

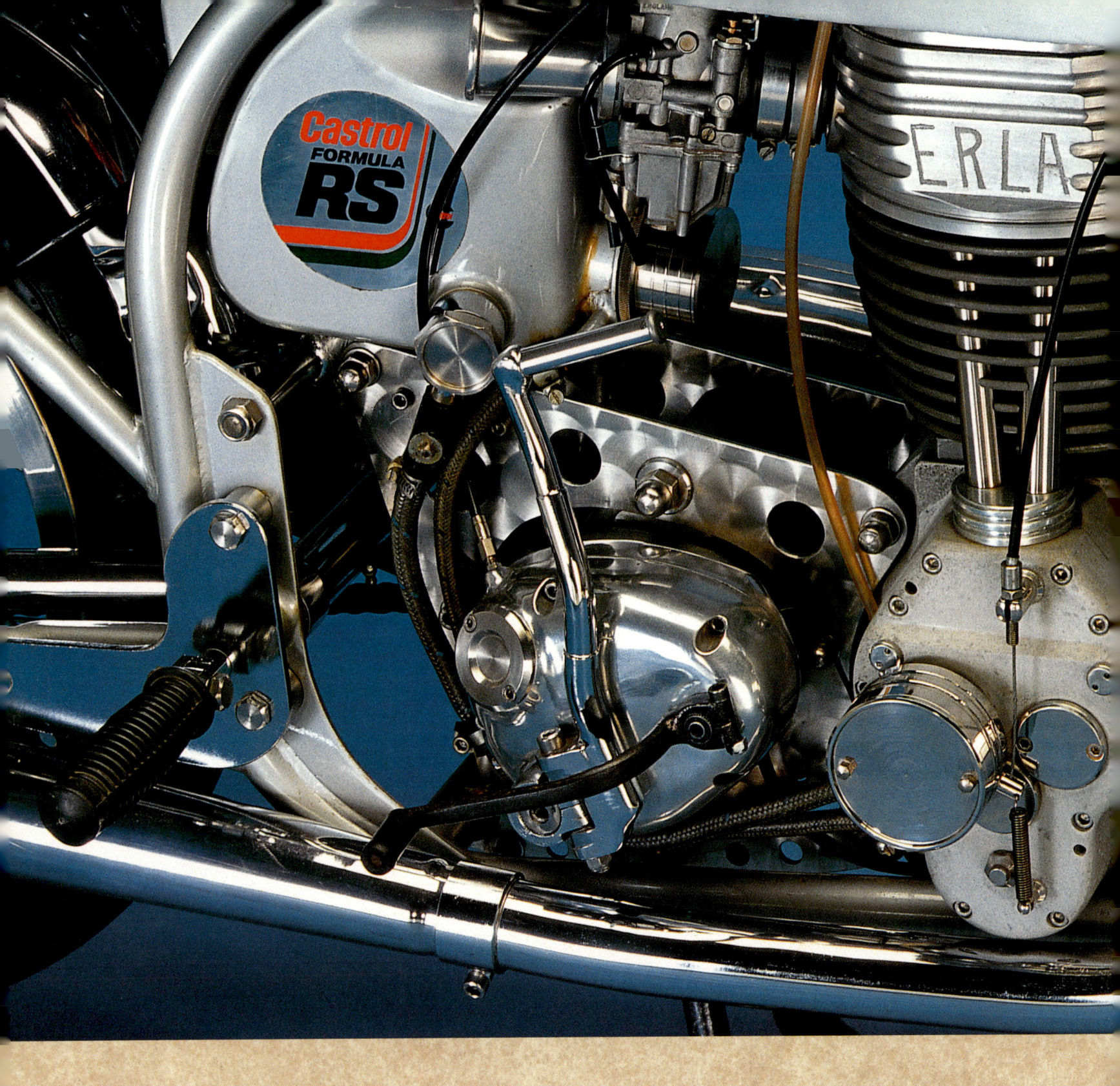

hours' work, there it was: the dream bike he had built himself, the Erla Special 500. A "one-lunger" with classic wire wheels was born. The cylinder head was machined out of solid metal, while the dimensions of 3 inch (80 mm) bore and 4 inch (99 mm) stroke promised loads of torque. The English-looking lady would produce 40 bhp on the road in her open-pipe version, but the rat-tat-tat of her exhaust was too loud for the ears of the official vehicle testers; 27 bhp had to suffice, accompanied by less noise.

Lawrenz had gone for the finest materials. The primary chain cover, with a Norton clutch and an alternator, is cast in elektron (a special light alloy), as is the crankcase. The connecting rod is made of titanium, and the crankshaft of chrome-molybdenum steel. A camshaft mounted in needle-roller bearings makes the similarly mounted rocker arms dance to the tune of the single cylinder.

The Erla has a Norton "Featherbed" frame and a four-speed gearbox of the same make. With 40 degrees advance, manual adjustment of the timing becomes a necessity when kick-starting; this explains the

88

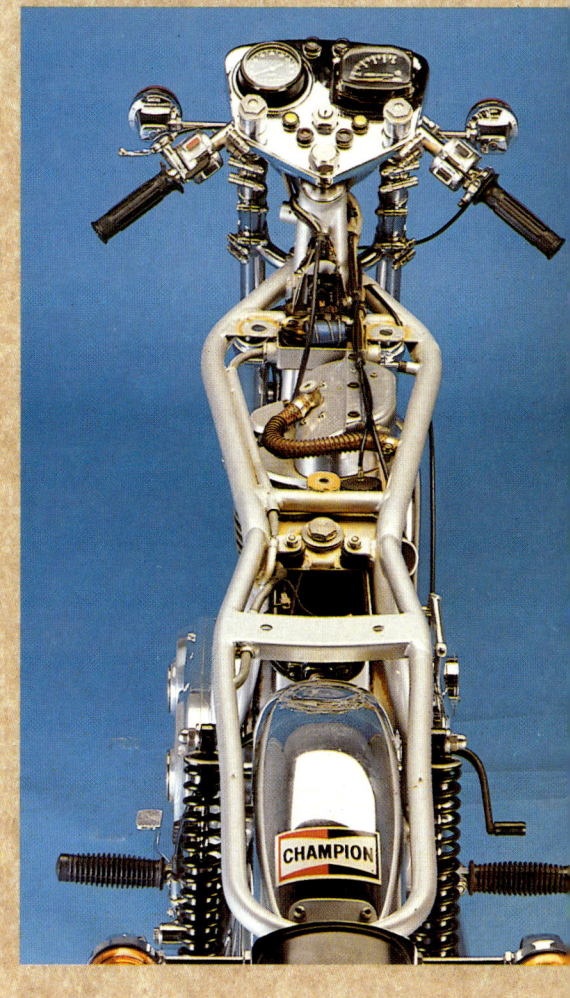

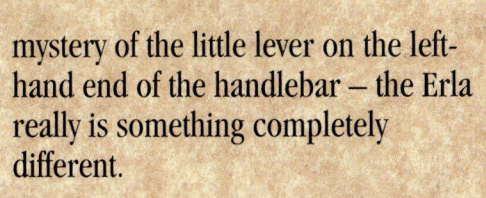

mystery of the little lever on the left-hand end of the handlebar – the Erla really is something completely different.

DATA SHEET	
Engine	Air-cooled single-cylinder four-stroke
Bore & stroke	3.1 x 3.9 ins (80 x 99 mm)
Capacity	30.5 cu ins (500 cc)
Power	38 bhp at 7,800 rpm
Transmission	Four-speed gearbox
Wheelbase	57 ins (1460 mm)
Frame	Steel double-cradle frame
Weight	352 lb (160 kg) with full tank
Maximum speed	93 mph (150 kph)
Production year	1989
Constructor	Erich Lawrenz

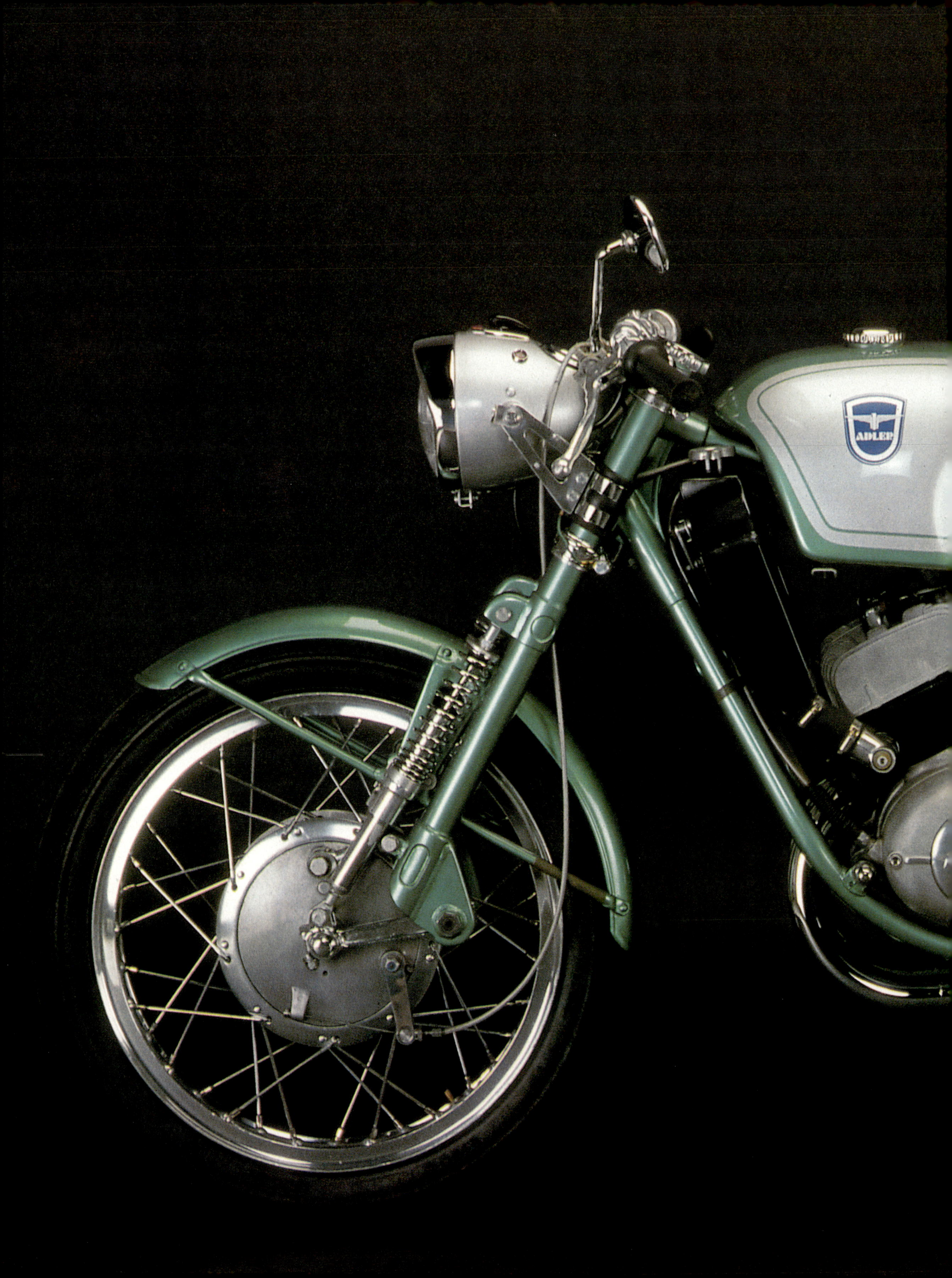
ADLER

The call of the eagle

When two Adler (meaning "eagle" in English) enthusiasts produce a new version of a classic sports machine, even an old two-stroke grows wings. The Adler, now with the refinements of modern technology, represents the summit of what can be achieved by skilled craftsmen.

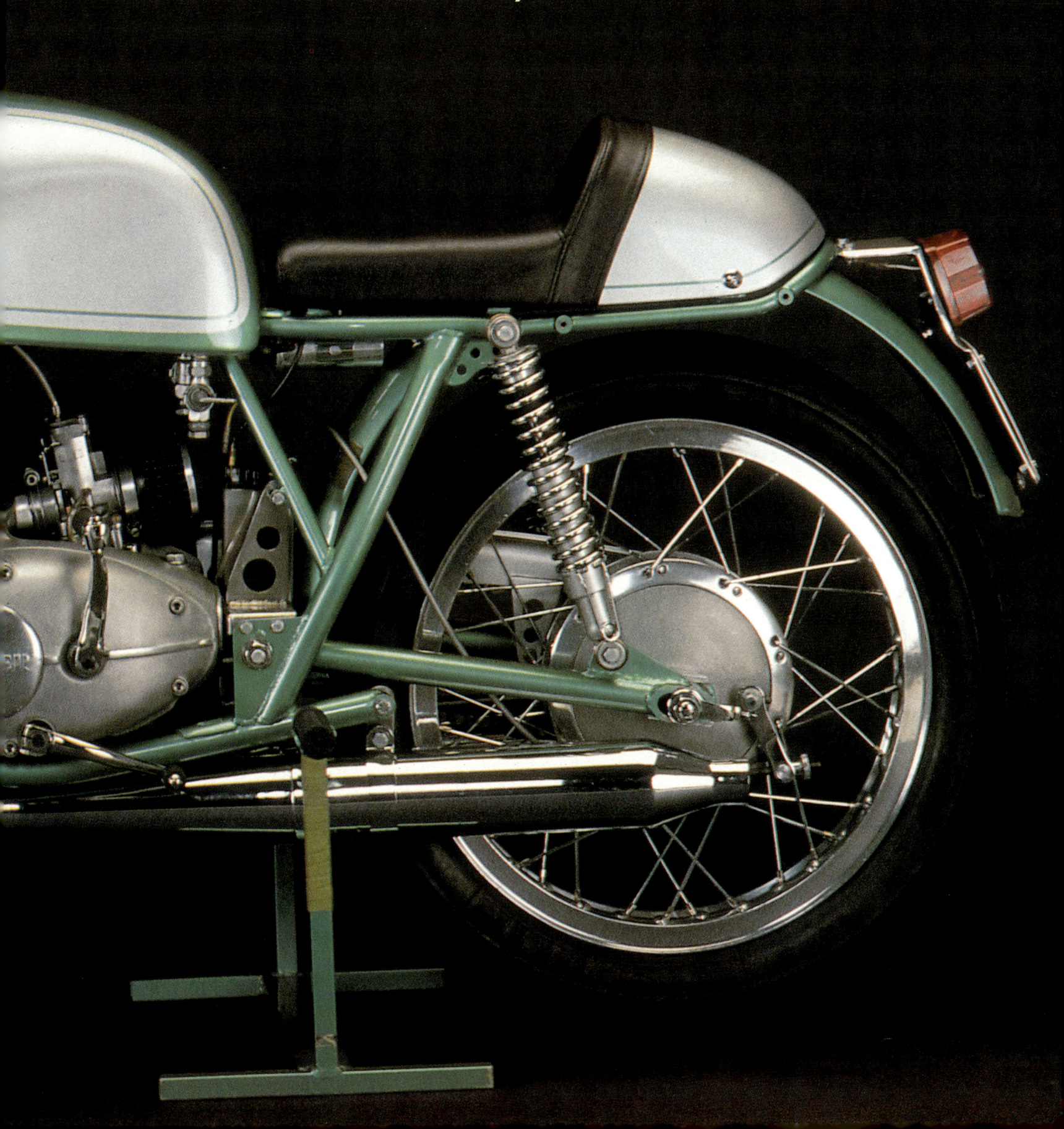

T he saying goes that too many cooks spoil the soup. But when building a motorcycle two people are better than one, especially when a mechanical engineer and a toolmaker get together. The ideas that one hatches can be implemented directly by the other on the workbench. That's why Christoph Schneider and Jupp Dolff make such a good team. These two fans of old Adler motorbikes met more than two years ago, and things got under way immediately. They wanted to build

92

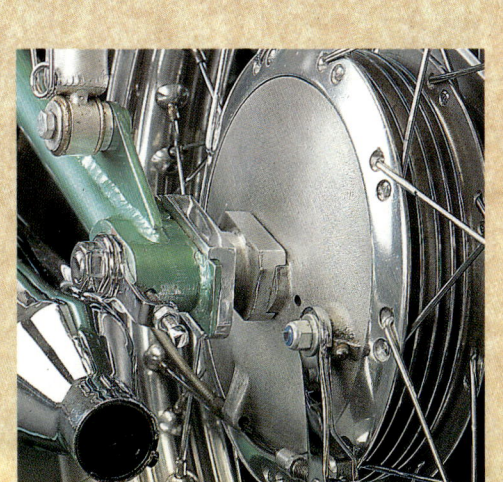

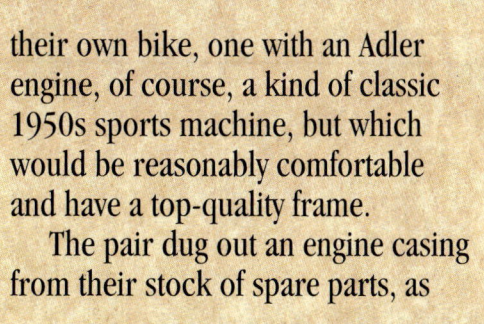

their own bike, one with an Adler engine, of course, a kind of classic 1950s sports machine, but which would be reasonably comfortable and have a top-quality frame.

The pair dug out an engine casing from their stock of spare parts, as well as the steering head from a 1953 Adler 250. Then began the great search for suitable parts. The front mudguard comes from a Honda SS 50, the headlight from a 1950s Hercules, and the suspension units from a Zündapp KS 125 – the list of used parts is long. The two men from Bonn devoted most of their efforts to the frame. With the help of frame calipers and a spirit level, they built the frame along exactly the same lines as that of the legendary Adler Rennsport (a sporty bike rather than a racer). The pretty forks, too, are inspired by the classic bike. Finally Schneider and Dolff converted the Adler's air-cooled cylinders to water cooling, and gave them air-cooled Yamaha cylinder

DATA SHEET

Engine	Water- and air-cooled twin-cylinder two-stroke
Bore & stroke	2.1 x 2.1 ins (54 x 54 mm)
Capacity	15 cu ins (250 cc)
Power	26 bhp at 7,500 rpm
Transmission	Four-speed gearbox
Wheelbase	52 ins (1320 mm)
Frame	Double cradle frame
Weight	297 lb (135 kg) with full tank
Maximum speed	93 mph (150 kph)
Production year	1989
Constructor	Christoph Schneider/ Jupp Dolff/Adler

heads. A Bing sports carburetor ensures the correct mixture; after all, one has to get the right power output. Around 26 bhp and a top speed of 93 mph (150 kph), with a weight of 297 lb (135 kg) is truly an impressive achievement. Incidentally, the pair have averted any argument as to who should ride the Adler. They are now building a second example.